Neurodiversity and Technology

T0385403

of related interest

Digital Kids
How to Balance Screen Time, and Why it Matters
Martin L. Kutscher
ISBN 978 1 78592 712 6
eISBN 978 1 78450 296 6

Video Modeling for Young Children with
Autism Spectrum Disorders
A Practical Guide for Parents and Professionals
Brenna Noland and Sarah Murray
ISBN 978 1 84905 900 8
eISBN 978 0 85700 638 7

NEURODIVERSITY and **TECHNOLOGY**

Neuroscience-led strategies for parents

Beatrice Moise

Jessica Kingsley Publishers
London and Philadelphia

First published in Great Britain in 2025 by Jessica Kingsley Publishers
An imprint of John Murray Press

1

Copyright © Beatrice Moise 2025

Front cover image source: iStockphoto® and Shutterstock®.

A CIP catalogue record for this title is available from the
British Library and the Library of Congress

ISBN 978 1 80501 225 2
eISBN 978 1 80501 226 9

Printed and bound in the United States by Integrated Books International

Jessica Kingsley Publishers' policy is to use papers that are natural,
renewable and recyclable products and made from wood grown in
sustainable forests. The logging and manufacturing processes are expected
to conform to the environmental regulations of the country of origin.

Jessica Kingsley Publishers
Carmelite House
50 Victoria Embankment
London EC4Y 0DZ

www.jkp.com

John Murray Press
Part of Hodder & Stoughton Ltd
An Hachette Company

The authorised representative in the EEA is Hachette Ireland,
8 Castlecourt Centre, Dublin 15, D15 XTP3, Ireland (email: info@hbgi.ie)

To all my neurodivergent people,
I see YOU!

Contents

Part 1: Understanding Neurodiversity, Neurodevelopment, and Technology

Part 2: Strategies to Support Neurodivergent Children with Technology Use

Disclaimer

I aim to provide others with information that helps promote a balanced, respectful, and enriched relationship between parents and children through education and teaching techniques. I also want to help anyone with a neurodivergent brain understand their relationship with tech and how they process and interpret information from technological advances differently.

I want to educate others on what I have spent the last few years of my professional life doing: helping others navigate around the challenges that come with having a neurodivergent brain. The information here is general and does not consider individual circumstances, objectives, or needs.

I reference autism and attention deficit hyperactivity disorder (ADHD) throughout this book but want to make sure that the reader understands that both are heterogeneous and there is not one single cause for autism or ADHD symptoms. My area of expertise and personal experience is those two specific areas of neurodiversity brain traits, with my children and myself expressing behavioral components of those diagnoses.

Autism spectrum disorders (ASDs) are unique and multifaceted neurodevelopmental conditions. Diagnosis stems from observing atypical behavior and focusing on impairments in social communication and interaction, as well as restricted, repetitive patterns of behavior. These challenges present opportunities for understanding and growth, paving the way for greater compassion and support.

ADHD is known to have a multifactorial causation, indicating that a combination of genetic, environmental, and neurobiological factors can influence its development. This complexity is further reflected in the vast diversity of symptoms and experiences among individuals with ADHD. These may include a variety of psychiatric comorbidities such as anxiety, depression, and oppositional defiant disorder.

The presentation of ADHD can vary widely, with some individuals exhibiting primarily inattentive symptoms while others may display predominantly hyperactive-impulsive symptoms or a combination of both. Neurocognitive impairments, such as difficulties with attention, executive functioning, and impulse control, further contribute to the heterogeneous nature of ADHD. Moreover, the developmental trajectories of individuals with ADHD can differ significantly, with some experiencing symptom remission in adulthood while others continue to struggle with symptoms throughout their lives. Finally, structural and functional brain anomalies, including alterations in brain regions involved in attention, executive function, and emotional regulation, have been observed in individuals with ADHD, adding another layer of complexity to the disorder. Before the implementation of any information that you read, you have to ask yourself if this applies to your life and if this aligns with what you can execute in your life. Please consider whether this advice is appropriate for you and your family when making decisions. This is general guidance and information based on personal and professional experience, including parenting philosophies, advice, and techniques. This book is the cumulation of years of helping hundreds of families better understand how to create an environment that allows them to enhance the technological advancement we have been afforded and manage the day-to-day struggles it can bring.

The information in this book is anecdotal and cannot and should not be construed as medical, psychological, or psychiatric advice. This book is a resource to help readers gain more education and empower them with the knowledge they did not previously possess, or to add to their library as an informational resource for their family or individuals who can benefit from it. The reader is responsible for ensuring that suggestions are appropriate for their well-being before using them.

Acknowledgments

I want to express my heartfelt gratitude to my wonderful children, Jake and Abby, for choosing me as their mother. The love and strength you have shown me have taught me invaluable lessons that no book or classroom could ever impart. You both inspire and motivate me in my journey as a parent and all aspects of my life. My love for you knows no bounds. LOVE YOU MOST!

My beloved Rubin, my cherished best friend, and husband, I am in awe of the incredibly beautiful and unimaginable journey we have shared. The moments we have experienced together have been nothing short of extraordinary. I am filled with love and appreciation for the extraordinary family that we have forged. Your support and companionship have been the cornerstones of my happiness. I am deeply grateful for your presence in my life. I cherish you deeply, my Boo.

I want to express my heartfelt gratitude to all the families who opened their homes and lives to me over the years. Your stories and experiences taught me invaluable lessons about the commonalities we share as human beings. Your willingness to be open and vulnerable has been a privilege, and I am deeply honored that you trusted me to provide guidance on parenting.

Thank you for allowing me to be a part of your parenting journey and for the opportunity to help you navigate the unique challenges and joys of raising your children.

To the reader of this book: Thank you immensely!

Preface

Technology: friend or foe? The response to that question varies from person to person. Some view technology as their adversary, while others see it as this life-changing and life-saving evolution of human development. I imagine the caveperson who started the first fire was probably thrown into the burning heat, the fire being seen as dangerous and needing to be eradicated immediately. Is fire dangerous? Absolutely! However, we have learned how to use and manipulate it to our advantage with proper knowledge. Continuous exposure and education have allowed us to see how fire can be used for warmth, food, and protection, to name a few.

Technological changes and advancements are viewed as chronicles of society's development, whereas cell phones and smart devices are often seen as adversaries—and so, with technology, we feel we are in a constant battle between good and evil. Technology was created to enhance lives, not ruin them. Some techs have been life-changing and life-saving for certain populations of the neurodivergent community; augmentative and alternative communication (AAC) devices, for example, have given so many individuals a voice when that hadn't been an option before. So, what happened? How did we get to this warfare with technology? The truth is that technology is evolving faster than we can adapt to it. Parents often introduce technology too early and without rules around navigating it safely. Technology is defined as applying scientific knowledge to help ease the quality and enhance the life of the human species—although it can also be used to do harm—meaning anything that can change or manipulate the environment is a technological advancement. We have discovered tools from ancient humans that are deemed technological inventions that date back to around 3 million years ago. So yeah, technology is not new; however, digital technology is. Digital tech uses electronic tools to stream communication quickly, store and process information, and gain access to resources from all around the world. Can we say "mind blown" for a moment? And it has only been around since the 1970s, in the Information Age. The Information Age is characterized by our ability to control and access information through personal computers. If our first attempt at technology was 3 million years ago, and the digital age only started 53 years ago, it's clear to me we don't have enough information on digital tech not to take precautions and dig further into the impact it can have.

Technology is responsible for our species' advancement and economic growth but also has adverse effects. These negative effects can be managed if we treat tech with the respect it deserves and do not assume that a child will automatically know what to do when faced with these tech issues. While it may seem like kids are born to navigate tech easily, they are not. Technology is designed to adapt to us, to learn what we like, think, and want; we are not built to adapt to tech. Teaching yourself and your child to interact with tech will ensure proper usage. *Neurodiversity and Technology* is the guide to help you successfully navigate that world.

I spent a few years observing people's relationships with technology and how parents navigate that world with their children. I have seen first-hand how parents can struggle to implement changes and maintain rules, which can be particularly hard to adhere to once your child leaves young childhood and enters early adolescence. My approach to this topic is different because I do not just want to tell you the pros and cons of technology and the many uses it has. I also want to tell you about the neuroscience involved in your brain that makes it hard for kids to detach and how, I hope, you can implement changes based on this newfound knowledge. Education is a powerful tool for life; understanding the why behind the behavior can help you create rules you can easily follow based on this new understanding.

I am a very proud neurodivergent individual, and so are my entire family. We see technology as a place of safety to learn how to interact with the neurotypical world that we often feel excluded from. We also use technology for entertainment and connection; dancing with my kids to regulate our nervous system has been a family tradition for 13 years. Learning that singing can facilitate the vagus nerve to stimulate electrical impulses to the brain was incredibly impactful in my life and in parenting neurodivergent children.

I want to educate you on how to use technology safely and effectively. This includes how certain neurotransmitters, like dopamine, serotonin, and oxytocin to name a few, and hormones like melatonin and cortisol are impacted by certain screen habits. The difficulties we all have go beyond our ability to control our impulses; biological components can also be involved.

This book is not intended only for young children and those who parent them, it's for everyone who wants a better understanding and more control over their abilities to monitor their behaviors and how they interact with tech, the relationship they have with it, and what they can do to enhance it or make changes to improve it for their well-being. Through reading this book, I hope you come to better understand the underlying cause of what happens before, during, and after you interact with technology in all facets of that interaction. We have learned a lot about the brain, and although there is still so much to uncover, we have learned how to utilize other means of information to educate ourselves on what we are doing and what we have done regarding tech.

The brain continues to mature well into your mid-20s, and neuroplasticity allows you to learn information throughout your lifetime. The neurodivergent brain develops at different rates. MRI (magnetic resonance imaging) studies on neurodivergent individuals have shown that parts of the brain that maintain language processing work differently for people diagnosed with dyslexia. I have dyslexia, and I concur. As a person with ADHD and two children with ADHD, I can also say that I have seen how executive functioning develops in a different and unique pattern. Being neurodivergent gives us the freedom not to be tied down to neurotypical norms. If you are a new parent of a young child and want to create preventative measures: excellent. And of course, for parents of teenagers and young adults, it's simply not too late to re-educate yourself or your child. If you are reading this at 45 years old to learn more about your brain: good for you—it's never too late. So wherever you are on the spectrum of brain development and knowledge-seeking, this book was designed, curated, and researched for you. Happy reading!

PART 1

Understanding Neurodiversity, Neurodevelopment, and Technology

Chapter 1

Neurodiversity and UNIQUE Parenting

What Is Neurodiversity?

Neurodiversity is an umbrella term coined by Australian sociologist Judy Singer in 1997 (Singer, 1998). Since then, the term has evolved into a movement that includes many individuals and is not just limited to autism. When I talk about neurodiversity, people often think primarily about autism, and sometimes ADHD is thrown into the mix, but rarely do I get people with anxiety to identify as neurodiverse. Once I explain the behavior behind the feeling or emotional state, it usually clicks, and that's when the person says, "I had no idea." I also believe there's a stigma behind identifying as a neurodivergent person, because it can also be taken to mean that you have a disability. I have found that certain people with neurodiversity, such as anxiety, ADHD, or depression, to name a few, do not necessarily see themselves as having a disability. I have never considered myself as someone with a disability, even though I have dyslexia, which is a learning disability. I view it as being just how my brain works. I now understand the difference, but I could not see it back then.

Neurodiversity is not the same thing as having a disability; you can be neurodivergent and have a disability or a mental illness, but they are not the same thing. When you purely have a disability, you have a condition that makes it more difficult or sometimes impossible to execute specific tasks and participate in certain daily activities. I know what you are thinking, especially if you, the person reading this, is neurodivergent yourself: how is this different from neurodiversity? The best way I can explain this is to give you an example.

My son has autism, anxiety, ADHD, and a communication disorder, and all those fall under the umbrella of neurodiversity; they significantly impact his way of interacting with the world, causing him to also have a disability because of the limitation he consistently experiences. His disability can be seen and identified by most people, but sometimes it can also be hidden, not intentionally. I'll go into that later.

I have ADHD and dyslexia, both under the neurodiversity umbrella again; however, I can interact with the general population with relative ease, now I have learned that I require accommodations for certain things, but they do not limit my interactions; therefore, I do not have a visible disability. But in writing, I have a learning disability that I learned to work through or masked greatly because I grew up when accommodations were not as easily accessible. So, I qualify under the term for an invisible disability. An invisible disability can be either a mental, physical, or neurological condition that you cannot see from the outside, but that can or does limit the individual's activities. Having an invisible disability also means that because it can't be seen, you are more likely to experience discrimination and doubt your own needs because you may question the validity of the issue yourself. Here is a list of some, but certainly not ALL, of the conditions that would cause someone to be identified as neurodivergent.

- Anxiety

- Attention deficit hyperactivity disorder (ADHD)

- Autism

- Bipolar disorder

- Borderline personality disorder

- Depression

- Down syndrome

- Dyscalculia (difficulty with math)

- Dysgraphia (difficulty with writing)

- Dyslexia (difficulty with reading)

- Dyspraxia (difficulty with coordination)

- Hyperlexia

- Intellectual disabilities

- Meares–Irlen syndrome

- Mental health conditions

- Obsessive-compulsive disorder

- Prader–Willi syndrome

- Sensory processing disorders
- Social anxiety
- Synesthesia
- Tourette syndrome
- Williams syndrome

I'd like to take a minute to highlight some words and their definitions that are used extensively in my world, and are frequently used in the wider world.

- *Neurodiversity* means that individuals are viewed more according to their brain activity and how unique their brains are, and isn't limited to one way of functioning. When talking about neurodiversity, it is essential to know some current terms that are often used.

- *Neurotypical:* The best way to understand this term is to consider it to mean the norm, or the majority of the population: people who do not require accommodations to understand the world, and can navigate society based on how it is intended.

- *Neurodiverse* is a descriptive term used to describe neurodivergent people.

- *Neurodivergence* is a noun that describes the individual atypical traits; so, for instance, my neurodivergence traits are ADHD and dyslexia.

- *Neurodivergent* is a description of the individuals who have neurodivergence.

The UNIQUE Parenting Approach

Neurodivergent families do not have the luxury of being able to purchase standard parenting books and apply the information to their child; it will not work. I have read many parenting books, and I can say they were filled with salient and useful information, as well as being well written. However, the application did not work for my child or family. I found most of the concepts to be the opposite of what was effective when it came to my children. I have also been given feedback from hundreds of families sharing the same sentiment. In response to this I created the UNIQUE parenting concept.

UNIQUE parenting is a mental mind shift to help you understand that what you are doing is not wrong, why it is not working for you, and how to try something different with the neurodivergent learner in order for them to feel heard and understood, thus decreasing the overall anxiety of negative feeling of parenting a child with unique learning needs.

What are the UNIQUE Parenting Stages?

- Understanding each situation is distinctive

- Not judging any style of parenting but looking at it differently

- Individualized teaching techniques to match strengths and abilities

- Quirky personalities that don't fit into a box

- Useful suggestions and ideas applied to daily parenting life

- Educating parents with extraordinary kids

UNIQUE parenting is a concept that I have found to be helpful when it comes to parenting a child that has learning differences, and it's important to say that these aren't stages you need to move through in a linear way. The way that a child achieves milestones and acquires knowledge is different, and therefore unique, and I wanted to make sure that the parenting the child receives is also unique, to match the way that child processes information. The stages reflect what to work on or improve but are not a requirement of what needs to be done before moving to the next stage. The stages are guidelines for individuals to understand themselves and/or their children better and see what areas may require more attention.

UNIQUE parenting is an approach that is applied throughout this book.

Stage 1: Understanding each Situation is Distinctive

UNIQUE parenting is a concept I created to match how I had to parent my children and to help the parents I work with understand what they are dealing with from a different perspective. There are six stages that you can practice in order to become more effective with your parenting strategies. The goal is to identify what requires attention, and to not focus on what you can already do well but on what you can do differently to enhance your relationship with your child. This idea can be summarized by the first stage: to understand. Knowledge is power; when it comes to children, the more understanding you have, the more manageable they become. Raising children who are neurodiverse is not easy, but it can also be enjoyable if you view each moment for what it is and not what it should be. When my children were younger, playdates were not enjoyable because the expectations of what they should look like were something that my kids could not meet; this made the early years difficult. Our family dynamic was peculiar to us, and with time I learned we had a clear and distinctive way of behaving and collaborating with others. Playdates needed to be less independent and involve more parental influence in order to be effective. For your family, this may not work; you may need something independent; the point is to realize that just because it's unique doesn't mean it is less.

Stage 2: Not Judging Any Style of Parenting but Looking at It Differently

I have spent over 15 years watching people with different backgrounds, social and economic statuses, races, and religions; you name it, I have seen it, and I have witnessed how they parent. If you have heard of the concept "I wish I could be a fly on the wall," well, I was the "Bea in the room," observing and taking in other environments vastly different from mine. I learned that judging parenting styles is an antiquated notion that does not factor in all the components that make these individuals parent the way they do. When it comes to parenting your child, your knowledge is also influenced by your own childhood experiences. The intention is well-meaning; you either want to parent your child as you were parented, or the opposite. This is a pattern I repeatedly noticed with clients, but it's not sustainable. I can't parent my children the way I was parented because they live in a completely different time and have access to things that as a child I thought were science fiction. Your knowledge of your child may also be limited due to circumstances that are out of your own control. In my case it was having a child with limited verbal capabilities to inform me of who they truly were. Not judging any parenting style but looking at parenting differently is based on the idea that these individuals mean well. If I can look behind the meaning but not judge their behavior, we can make significant progress that will benefit both parent and child. Examine what preconceptions you have about yourself and others when it comes to parenting, challenge those ideas to improve them, and shift those mindsets into something more productive. If you feel like you are being judged on how your family utilizes tech, this can impede your ability to do what is needed. Neurodivergent families sometimes use tech out of necessity, and others may judge this as bad parenting; the judgment can come from strangers and within the family, such as extended family members. If you are feeling or experiencing this form of judgment, remember that you are doing your best, and being judged or scrutinized will not change your overall goal of understanding and giving your child what they need.

Stage 3: Individualized Teaching Techniques to Match Strengths and Abilities

Neurodiverse children require certain things to be personalized; while this can be viewed as a weakness, I see it as a strength. When you adapt individualized teaching techniques to match strengths and abilities, you create a home or learning environment that is designed to help your child thrive. Technology is part of that learning environment; the rules that exist for everyone can be different from those you apply for your child. If you don't make decisions that are tailored to your family, they simply will not work, and if they do, it will only be for a while before they stop.

When I was trying to figure out how to teach my son anything, it was a journey, a journey I wrote about in *Our Neurodivergent Journey: A Child Like Mine* (Moise, 2022). I spent years observing what my son needed and what I needed to do in order for him to thrive because it was such a different road than I had previously experienced with other children and with how I learned and acquired information as a child. Jake learns with repetition and touch. He is a tactile learner, which means that he has to touch and feel something to learn it. He likes the multisensory approach. I would watch him do something new, and he would look at it, smell it, drop it, and manipulate it to get a sense of what it was and how it functioned. I had to figure out how to teach him using this learning style. You can't touch the number 1, so how would I teach counting? And you can't drop the letter A, so how could I teach reading? When teaching him to read and write I had to take a different approach, and I had to work on his strengths. His strength in this area happens to be patience and repetition. I had to use those skills to teach him about almost everything. He enjoys doing repetitive tasks, and when you can tag music to it, well, you have hit the goldmine. When you learn what your child's strengths are, you can start the process of teaching them about anything. Technology has allowed Jake to learn more efficiently because he can play a video repeatedly until he has absorbed the information in the way he does best.

Stage 4: Quirky Personalities That Don't Fit into a Box

If I had a dollar each time someone referenced me as weird or odd, especially in childhood, I could probably retire right now. As an adult, I don't get a lot of this, mostly due to the fact that I learned how to mask my ADHD traits; sometimes I am unaware that I am masking. *Masking* is a coping mechanism whereby, having been told many times that you are odd, you begin to create a character that is more accepted by the masses. Masking starts in childhood and is rooted in trauma. It was a trauma response for me. I developed a carefully curated personality that people would not see as too odd but was wittier and more interesting than I really was. After years of interpersonal work, I realized that some of my masking personality had become a big part of who I am, and I have made peace with that. However, when it came to my kids, I recognized that their quirky personalities are not something to help them adjust or change so that they are digestible to others, but to be amplified to allow them to be who they are designed to be. No one in my household fits "neurotypical" norms; we are all out-of-the-box thinkers and doers, and we celebrate that very fact.

Stage 5: Useful Suggestions and Ideas Applied to Daily Parenting Life

Once upon a time, I was the perfect parent; I can give you the exact timeline: from 2002 to 2008. I was the world authority on best parenting practices. I only had one problem, relatively minor, back then. I did not have children, NONE; I was not even married. But those are the years I spent in school learning about child development for both undergrad and grad school. The problem with learning about child development is that you can begin believing that every practice can be applied to any scenario and will work well. One of the greatest gifts I received was the ability to go inside homes to see how perfectly well-meaning practices can be completely ineffective because of the home environment and the individuals within the dwelling.

Fast forward a few years: when I had my children, I started to see why these tools that were being given to parents simply could not work. When my daughter was five years old, I thought creating a visual schedule for her would help her start her day. At this point, I created hundreds of schedules for families; they all seemed to love them and they worked. I already had a schedule for my son, and he LOVED it. Naturally, I thought this was going to be easy. Well, it wasn't at all. The intentions behind it were good, but the execution was not. For Abby, I needed to do the schedule with her. Her learning style was different from Jake's learning style. Task completion for her required body doubling, so a checklist was not going to be beneficial in this case. Body doubling is when a person works alongside someone else to complete a task that they may not find enjoyable; it helps with eliminating distraction, a trait high in my daughter and myself because we both have ADHD. In this circumstance, I had these great suggestions and ideas to apply to my daily parenting life, but it was not working, and I had to do something that was practical for my environment. I learned that the accommodation I needed to do for my child and myself was to teach her these skills over the weekend, and it was not something she was going to manage independently.

Stage 6: Educating Parents with Extraordinary Kids

Education is freedom; it gives us the opportunity to understand something previously a mystery; it is such a powerful tool to have when it comes to parenting. As parents and caregivers, we spend money on our children without thinking about it; sometimes, it is out of needs and necessity, and other times, it is because of wants, and it feels good to provide your child with something you did not have or wasn't accessible to you as a child. However, when it comes to education, learning who your child is is a key component to change. Figuring out a child is often left to other professionals. We will ask pediatricians, teachers, and therapists about who our children are, and in my experience working it out for ourselves is not often encouraged by professionals. I learn so much from kids; they have taught me things about who they are that could not be outsourced. Growing up, I often felt misunderstood in my home. I would look around me and think that these people did not match me or who I was on the inside; remember, I spent a tremendous amount of my energy masking, and this included masking in my home environment. When you become educated on who your child is, you free them and yourself. Unleashing this hidden power of connection is something you may not know is even possible, but it is. I educate others about neurodivergent people. That's my whole objective, and learning about how extraordinary your child is, this is only the beginning; wait until you see what they do with it!

In a true dyslexic and neurodiverse fashion, you do not have to implement the UNIQUE stages in the order they appear. If you want to start with educating yourself on how your child learns and allow that to be the conduit to understanding your situation, then do that. These are tools to be used as needed, not laws that can't be broken.

Chapter 2

Understanding the Science

Before we get started, let's find out more about how our brains are made up, and how we can work with our hypothalamus to help us understand why it's hard to create routines when it comes to screens, and how to tackle this. While we would love to believe that we are acting out of our own volition and desires, the scientific truth is that we are not; we are responding internally to an external component that is being received by our brain. The hypothalamus is an area of the brain that keeps your body balanced. You can think of it as a check-and-balance system of the brain; it ensures that things are in a state of *homeostasis*, that is, a self-regulating process that maintains equilibrium. The hypothalamus also produces the hormone dopamine. Dopamine has been quite the buzzword recently; while most people are not fully aware of all of its functions, they do have an understanding that it involves the reward center of the brain.

Dopamine has many functions. It gives you feelings of satisfaction, pleasure, and motivation. Dopamine controls memory, mood, sleep, learning, concentration, movement, and other body functions. When we interact with screens, the dopamine response is one of pleasure and motivation. The effects of dopamine can lead to problematic moods that impact the child's behavior.

When your child wants to play a game, they have to get motivated to play that game. Dopamine is released before they even start playing that game because that is how they get the motivation to play it. Sustaining motivation is another act of dopamine, because the chemical is released to ensure that they stay engaged; this component is the pleasure aspect. Finally, when they reach the next level of the game, there is another release, giving a feeling of satisfaction. As a parent, the way you see dopamine manifesting is mood regulation, because you can see your child go up and down with their emotions during this interaction. They can be happy one minute and in some deep rage the next, all while doing something that seems to be enjoyable. This is the role dopamine plays in on-screen gaming. To be clear, your brain uses dopamine in the same way for tasks that are not screen related. However, the frequency with which children interact with screens differs from chores, yard work, or homework. They go through this loop every day, often for hours at a time, and this interaction does exist in another aspect of their life, as illustrated in the diagram below.

When you hand a child a device, this is what happens in the brain. The same thing happens when you hand a toddler a tablet. Without being aware of it, you are strengthening a neurological connection so when that toddler turns into a teenager, they have developed this habit over the years, and it's not easy to stop.

Blum *et al.* (2008) state that "people with ADHD have at least one defective gene, the DRD2 gene that makes it difficult for neurons to respond to dopamine."

Blum *et al.* (2008) also state that:

Molecular genetic studies have identified several genes that may mediate susceptibility to attention deficit hyperactivity disorder (ADHD). A consensus of the literature suggests that when there is a dysfunction in the "brain reward cascade," especially in the dopamine system, causing a low or hypo-dopaminergic trait, the brain may require dopamine for individuals to avoid unpleasant feelings. This high-risk genetic trait leads to multiple drug-seeking behaviors, because the drugs activate release of dopamine, which can diminish abnormal cravings.

Old School Loop

Desire to watch TGIF ↦ Wait until Friday ↦ Watch TGIF ↦ Internal reward while watching TGIF ↦ Crash when TGIF ends ↦ Loop closes

New Age Loop

Desire to play game ↦ Plays game ↦ Internal reward for playing game ↦ Leveling up creates an external reward of playing game ↦ Crash from game completion ↦ Start the process all over without break ↦ Loop starts back up

My behavioral reward loop as a child in the 1990s versus my children's behavioral loop in the 2020s

Kriete and Noelle (2015) state that the alterations in dopaminergic transmission could be the cause of "reduced motivation to pursue social interactions," since the brain of autistic individuals could register these activities as "not rewarding." This reduced motivation also leads to reduced social experience.

Okay, now that you have the scientific perspective, this will help you understand that it's more than just implementing behavioral changes. These are changes happening in the structure of the brain. As a mother of a child with autism and another one with ADHD, this lets me know that dopamine has a direct impact on their behaviors. I must factor this in when it comes to a dopamine-inducing activity. As a neurodivergent person myself, I have to understand how it also impacts me in order to make proper changes for my family as a whole. Scientific research has told us that dopamine and the neurodivergent mind interact with each other in a way that is not typical, and why wouldn't we want to have an atypical brain? I love having an atypical brain because I love seeing the world the way I do, but I also have to be mindful of how my atypical brain can react to the stimuli I am engaged with. I also have to be highly cognizant of how these stimulations are impacting my children.

Behavioral changes are designed to help you gain control over something that is hard to manage. They're not designed to get rid of the hard-wired mechanisms in your system but as a guardrail to help you stay in line and not deviate from the original framing. They also bring you back to where you should be if you are heading in the wrong direction. Children will always fall out of the alignment they are learning; part of learning is making mistakes. You can't learn if you do not make a mistake because you won't know what to change or how to do it another way. However, a part of your job is to be there for the active learning aspect and help them make adaptations when and where needed. Kids are incapable of doing this themselves because although the driving force to get them to act works as it should, the external environment impacts how those internal mechanisms react. We did not have this level of interference in previous generations. At the same time, technology is not new; access to pleasure-seeking entertainment being so readily available is new and it is going to be a struggle for the neuro-divergent brain.

What Is Serotonin?

The presence of the neurotransmitter serotonin in your brain regulates your mood, specifically giving you a happy and calm mood. When your brain secretes the typical level of serotonin, you get the feeling of being focused and able to tackle the day. When you have low levels of serotonin, you may feel less agreeable.

I talk to families about serotonin when it comes to managing the negative behaviors they may experience with getting off screens or if their child doesn't want to do anything outside the device. Connection is a big part of how the nervous brain builds relationships. When my son was younger, and he was in therapy five days a week, we had different therapists throughout that time, and while he would "do" the task being asked, his progress was nothing compared to the relationship he had with one of his therapists. She and he had this beautiful bond and relationship that made him feel calm, and he could do tasks that he hadn't been able to do prior to this. I saw how this played out because when that therapist had to leave, he did not make the same progress with any of the others. The others were just as talented and skillful, but it was always different. There is something greater at play here; this is beyond a child working with a therapist. A child's brain responds to his or her therapist with an internal reward that can't be matched. Johnson *et al.* (1999) state that better mood is associated with higher blood serotonin levels. Two other studies found that greater prolactin release in response to fenfluramine was associated with more positive mood (Zald & Depue, 2002 and Flory *et al.*, 2004, cited in Young, 2007).

What does this mean to you as a parent, or what does it mean for your child? This clearly states the strong correlation between a positive mood and a positive relationship with another person. When your child is on their device, they may form positive relationships with the people or personalities behind the screen, making them feel calm and happy. They may not know why they feel this way, but it doesn't change the fact that they feel it and, therefore, are going to try to seek more and more of it. A child refusing to get off a device is more complex than them just not wanting to get off the device. I want you to see it from this perspective. Instead, you are asking them to break a positive connection with something that brings them calmness and happiness, and their brain will not respond positively to something like that because does that even make sense? If you are telling your child to break this connection and not have another and, dare I say it, a better connection, they are not going to willingly comply.

When you better understand the chemicals involved in your child's behavior, it empowers you to tackle it from another angle. Neurodivergent people require a whole-body approach when it comes to interventions; we do well when most of our needs are met instead of a few. In our home, any time devices are put away, there's an activity that my kids are looking forward to doing; the way it works for us is that when my children are in the middle of their device time, and I say "Family game night at 6:00 pm," they have a catalog of positive family interactions to recall, making the activity something to look forward to doing, and know there will be moments feeling happy and calm, but most importantly, they are also aware of the calmness that is associated with these activities. If you are wondering how this is different from dopamine, let me clarify.

Dopamine is motivation and rewards. When we are about to have family game nights, my kids need motivation to get off their devices, and they understand that there's a reward coming, and that reward might be one of them dominating at a family game. Serotonin assists with being calm, focused, and happy, and that's the feeling they get when they are in the middle of the family game night. In other words, dopamine gets to want to do the game night, and serotonin keeps them in the game night. These neurotransmitters work together, and we should look at how they work together so we can work together as people.

Your child may have already developed a positive relationship with these neurotransmitters but in a negative way. Neurodivergent individuals are prone to dysregulated systems and rollercoaster moods, and therefore we are always searching for ways to self-soothe or self-regulate. I can wake up in the best mood, but if my favorite and most precious tea mug is not available, this can easily ruin my day. Devices can offer us immediate respite, but we also need to know how to find other streams of calmness and joy. The avenue for this exists in a healthy interactive dynamic that is built on a relationship in which family time can be enjoyable, and a break from screens is not immediate torture.

Routines take time to build and require consistency; pulling your child away without having a backup plan is not going to work, and telling them to find something else to do that they enjoy is also not going to work. Remember, the goal here is to work with science and develop a system that will enhance the way your child's neurotransmitters are working and enhance your daily interactive dynamic.

What Is the Reward System?

Neurodivergent people have a relationship with rewards that is not very well understood. When my son was younger, and we would try to figure out ways to motivate him to do something, he was not responsive to the reward. I had to tell the therapist that he doesn't really care for rewards; if he wants to do it, he will, and if he doesn't, he won't. Sometimes, he doesn't want to do it, but he will do it anyway; no rewards are needed. He is still like this, but with him, even if he doesn't want to do something, there's an internal driver that will make him do the task even if it's not desired. My son does not have the typical autistic response that I have encountered; in that way, he's atypical with his response to rewards. Now, don't get me wrong, he loves rewards, but he will not work for them. Maybe it's something I did in his early childhood with my parenting that developed this relationship. I am not quite sure, but I also see a bit of temperament in this equation as well. He has that type of personality that spends a great deal of time analyzing a situation prior to making a decision. If I were to guess, I would say that he is an introverted thinker with a personality trait of agreeableness similar to his father's, but with an added layer of mystery.

My daughter's relationship with reward is extraordinary, and she loves validation. If you want her to do something, you ask her to do it and tell her how great she is at it, but this way of being rewarded is limited to tasks. When it comes to school-work, she is incredibly self-motivated. She has the desire to do well and likes doing well. She reminds me of my relationship with school and life with this desire to be perfect, obviously fueled by anxiety. In the terms of Carl Jung, she is an Introverted Sensation with a personality trait of Conscientiousness.[1] While it may look like she is driven internally to do well, and she is, there's also an additional layer of people-pleasing. Her grades function as an external good job.

Both of my children showcase the different ways they process rewards, and I have to factor that into my parenting and how I treat them. Since they both respond in a way that is unique to them, I had to think of ways to create incentives that were also unique to each of them. When I think about what motivates me and what rewards my behavior, there's something in my brain that decides when something is a high reward and when it is not. The amygdala influences reward. A smaller amygdala can lead to various things, including anxiety and depression, and ADHD

---

1   Carl Jung, one of my favorite psychologists, came up with a theory of personality that bridges the gap between the conscious and unconscious mind. Jung believed that people experience the world using four psychological functions: sensation, intuition, feeling, and thinking. For more detail, see Jung (1981).

individuals tend to have smaller amygdala volumes. This might explain why rewards are different for the neurodivergent brain and why it's hit or miss at times.

Preparing to write this book, I had all the motivation to do it; I wanted to do it, and I was excited to write about a topic I was passionate about and believed would help the neurodivergent population. This book is also helpful for neurotypicals, so double the reward. It's helpful for everyone of all ages. This very fact motivated me in all aspects. I sat down to write, and in two months, I had written 20,000 words. I know this because I made a chart to keep myself on track. I was making significant progress, and then my brain decided I was way ahead and I could take a break and do other meaningless tasks. This started my ADHD procrastination loop.

My ADHD procrastination loop is something I have lived with my entire life; when I was younger, the way I coped with this was perfectionistic. When I received an assignment or task, I handled it immediately because, in my mind, if it's early, it can't be late. I use the same tactic as an adult. The minute I get asked to do something, if possible, I do it right away. However, depending on the task, I may not able to complete it immediately in one sitting; a task like writing a book cannot be completed in one sitting. I am sure someone out there has done this, but this was out of my wheelhouse of capabilities. Niermann and Scheres (2014) indicated that there is a positive correlation between ADHD-related symptoms of inattention and general procrastination in a sample of well-functioning students. This preliminary finding may stimulate more research on the possible relation between procrastination and symptoms of ADHD in individuals with a clinical diagnosis.

I created a chart that was supposed to motivate me to complete this book with a daily writing schedule, but I decided I should have weekly goals instead, which could have been more effective if I could stick to it. So, I made the final decision to have a monthly goal; after all, I had months to complete the book. This was an epic failure. As a neurodivergent person, I have learned that sometimes rewards that worked in the past will not always work in the present. But there's a particular reward that has never failed me or let me down, and that is procrastination. Procrastination is a reward to me; when I wait until the last minute, I will get whatever I need to complete done. It's worked for years, and it has yet to fail me. I have a backup plan, and that backup is that I do it early and ahead of time. When I wrote my first book, I completed the manuscript from beginning to end prior to submission. When you are submitting a book proposal, you are typically given time to complete the manuscript, but I knew I had to finish this book ahead of time. However, this book is on a topic I love, and I wanted to do tons of research on it. I could not commit to the research and everything prior to getting the book approved, so I waited before writing. When my submission was approved, I immediately started to write, which was the motivation. And then I lost motivation and waited months before writing again.

How is all this related to tech? Well, while I need the motivation to do desired tasks and things that I will be happy to have completed, my relationship with technology is different. I am always motivated to be on my device. The device itself is the reward. I am motivated by having it without having to do anything or get anything in return. In fact, the idea of having access to all the information I can conjure up is what makes the device the reward for my ADHD brain. Most people have an immediate relationship with technology.

As a parent, you can now understand that your child may be motivated to do other things, and they may certainly have the desire to get them done, but their brain may not produce what they need at the moment to get that thing done. I have seen that "tech before tasks" is not a good idea. Remember, tech is an immoderate reward; why would I work when I already got the reward? In my work, I have seen parents say that technology is the only thing that gets their children to do the work. Instead, I want them to see that tech is the thing keeping the child from doing the work. When I need to get my chores completed, I use tech to get me motivated, and that tech is auditory, meaning I listen to music. I get the release of dopamine that is required to motivate me to do laundry, but if I sit down to watch a video clip, it's a wrap that laundry is not going to happen, at least not today.

Audio technology via music is a great way to access dopamine in order for you to become motivated to accomplish tasks. Technology can work with you to gain access to rewards, but it has to be the right type of tech. Visual tech often serves as a distraction and is not beneficial when it comes to finding motivation to do tasks, whereas music that can be listened to via headphones or devices can help you gain access to releasing rewards in the brain. Music is my go-to reward and motivation to get tasks done, and I have seen it to be effective in most of my clients and highly effective with my kids. When they were younger, I put everything in a song when I asked them to do a task, and it worked. Music-evoked pleasure is driven, among other things, by its intrinsic ability to induce feelings such as anticipation and euphoria.

Other options need to be visited for you and your child; music might not work, and finding the right type of music might also be a challenge. Lyrical music helps me facilitate or initiate a task, but instrumentals help me focus on mental tasks and get tasks completed. My daughter prefers the sound of a crowd walking around or a busy train station or coffee shop when she is engaged in homework or studying; I find that distracting, but for her, it's helped her focus. My son listens to lyrical music when he is doing his homework. I would be too busy singing along. It would never work for me, but it works for him.

Now that you understand the reward center and how it can be utilized, your next task is to find the reward that will work for you. When I think back to when the therapist was trying to find the reward that was going to work for my son, she never brought up music as an option. She asked me if he liked a device, and at that point, I said we would not use that as a reward because I wanted him to have a relationship that was healthy with his device. I am glad that I did.

Sit down with your child and discover what reward is going to work best. Consider what reward you responded well to. What works for others may not work for your neurodivergent family, or it may work initially but stop at some point. And that might be because that is not what is needed now, and it's time to circulate a new form of reward. When writing this book, by the time I got close to the end of the year, I had completed 20,000 more words in less than a week. The motivation for me was that I ran out of time, and the reason was I wanted the information to be available. I revisited that chart I created and believed would help me, and laughed because even though I made it months ago, my brain knew exactly what I would do and what would work.

Chapter 3

Neurodiversity and Technology

What is human development, anyway? Depending on who you ask, the answer will vary. In this context it is about growth and development, and the different stages we move through over a lifespan.

Human development can be broken down into the following stages:

1. Infancy

2. Toddler

3. Childhood (3 to 11 years old)

4. Adolescence or teenage (12 to 18 years old)

5. Adulthood

My objective in taking a lifespan approach to the topic of technology use is to be inclusive of all my neurodivergent community and to create a resource that is of help and interest to most, if not all.

Looking at my children, I am always impressed by them. From the most straightforward task, I marvel at how they navigate through it. When they were toddlers, I would watch them use things as tools to either get something or get themselves into trouble. And I would watch to see how quickly they would either come to me for help or walk away from the problem. Even before they were born, I was fascinated by the different developmental stages of pregnancy. I was so intrigued by how this developing person would go from one thing to another each week. I was fascinated by neurodevelopment and still am. *Neurodevelopment* is the term we use to describe how the brain is developing its neurological pathways and how these pathways can then influence different functions such as memory, social skills, intellectual function, reading ability, focus, and attention skills.

The brain's development is a multifaceted and lengthy progression that begins roughly two weeks after conception and continues into early adulthood, encompassing a period of about 20 years. While brain development extends into early adulthood, the early childhood phase is pivotal in laying the foundation for a healthy and well-functioning brain.

The development of the nervous system is most pronounced during the early years of life, involving the intricate establishment of the brain's structure and functioning. This complicated process relies on the progressive formation of synaptic networks that connect nerve cells and the ongoing refinement of neurons, optimizing their adaptations for specific roles within these networks. Significantly, this developmental process extends well into adolescence, underlining the prolonged and dynamic nature of neurological development. As parents, we must recognize that while a child can do some incredible things, they still have an underdeveloped brain that requires guidance and input. In late childhood, children can seem to develop more mature ideas and concepts, and while I do not want to dismiss a child who might be more aware and have a better sense of self than when they were younger, I cannot get over the fact that a 12-year-old still has a lot of developing they need to go through. As parents and caregivers, we get to shape the experiences that a child will have, and when we outsource that to technology without prior guidelines and understanding, we risk shaping a young person's perception in a direction that was probably not intended. However, with care, we can also outsource it in a more positive way that can be beneficial and help decrease frustrations. I have learned first-hand how it can be shaped in that direction.

Parents are mainly concerned with brain development and how technology may negatively impact a developing child's social, emotional, and psychological well-being. Brain development continues into young adulthood, which can offer parents peace of mind that it's not too late to make changes or create new protocols. The brain processes information in a hierarchy of needs. It starts with the basic foundation and increases with age. However, the neurodivergent brain does not follow this pattern. Child development in neurodiversity tends to develop differently. As a parent of a neurodivergent child, you must eliminate the idea that there is a standard, and your child must adhere to it. There is no standard for human development. For example, the fact that your child may have been silent for years and then started to speak like a little professor should be proof that language development may not be as simple as we thought, or maybe your child bypassed crawling and went straight into walking, as my son did, and he has never looked back.

In regard to technology, your parental objective is to help your child with the information they have not acquired and to teach them how to manage behaviors to enhance their standard of living: a standard that may be different from what you experienced as a child. The focus must be on teaching healthy tech behavior to help your child learn how to create a balanced relationship with technology.

Did You Know?

In an article called "The myth of the normal brain," Thomas Armstrong states:

> People diagnosed with autism spectrum disorder (ASD), for example, appear to have strengths related to working with systems (e.g., computer languages, mathematical systems, machines) and in experiments are better than control subjects at identifying tiny details in complex patterns.
>
> People with dyslexia have been found to possess global visual-spatial abilities, including the capacity to identify "impossible objects" (of the kind popularized by M. C. Escher), process low-definition or blurred visual scenes, and perceive peripheral or diffused visual information more quickly and efficiently than participants without dyslexia...
>
> In the field of intellectual disabilities, studies have

noted heightened musical abilities in people with Williams syndrome, the warmth and friendliness of individuals with Down syndrome, and the nurturing behaviors of persons with Prader-Willi syndrome. (Armstrong, 2015)

These examples of the neurodivergent brain are the reason why we have to learn how to teach our kids about tech usage and embrace technology to give them a future with tech. This book will provide practical tools you can implement in your home, school, or any other environment where tech is available for your family. In addition, it will help you understand the neurodivergent mind and how its relationship with technology is something that can be nurtured in a positive way.

Neurodiversity, Technology, and Parenting

Neurodiversity and tech are things that I have always wanted to write about because of my relationship with tech and how it has impacted my life. However, it was indeed my son who inspired me to see all the positive benefits that can be attached to it and how proper implementation of tech can be beneficial to families that are struggling to find a way to communicate with their child, or whose child is struggling to find a way to connect with peers. My daughter highlighted the dangers of tech because of the nature of typical social interactions in girls; I quickly saw how school conversations and topics were not limited to the school environment but could be brought home and allowed to ruminate for weeks at a time. I am one of the lucky ones who implemented a check and balance system early, allowing me to catch things before they could go to another level. Unfortunately, I know far too many others who did not have the same opportunity.

I wanted to approach this topic with caution because of my work experience. I saw how families were struggling to find a balance, and once tech was introduced, it was impossible to go back. Once something went wrong, the profound psychological impact it had on both the child and family was, at times, devastating. What was the solution? How could I teach about tech and its dangers when I was fully aware that this mountain was far steeper than I had previously imagined?

I approached this concept in the only way I knew: to break down complicated concepts into small digestible bites and create visual representations and examples that families could apply to their lives. I had clients who shared with me that they never had a friend in the 3D world, social settings brought them an incredible amount of anxiety, and the constant rejection was too hard to endure; in the virtual world, they were king, accepted and adored by all. On the other hand, I have had children who experience such extreme levels of virtual bullying that they felt rejected and had to live with and endure an experience being played out repeatedly for all to see.

How can such two extremes exist? And what can we do about this? The neurodivergent aspect comes into play when these same scenarios are being played out and now you add a child with anxiety who can't move on from this interaction, or a child who has difficulties understanding the social complexities of the 3D world who thinks that maybe their 100th time will be the time when they will make a friend, or a child whose current school environment may not be the best fit and that's why they are struggling. After lots of research and tons of doubts about how to present this information, I decided to teach people about:

- how to model tech use

- creating spaces in their environment that are tech-free

- coming up with rules for both parents and children

- what to do when they are done with using tech for the day or evening

- handling that transition when they must come off

- learning and understanding some of the neuroscience occurring with tech usage

- how to travel with tech.

These pillars I felt were most important, and the ones I faced consistently in my professional career as a coach, and also as a parent and mother of two neurodivergent children.

Strategies to Support Neurodivergent Children with Technology Use

PART 2

Strategies to Support Neurodivergent Children with Technology Use

Chapter 4

Modeling, Inclusion, and Exclusion

When it comes to modeling good examples for our children, we usually have no idea how hard this is and how much they watch us. I have this habit of picking items off the ground with my toes; I do not know why, I just know that I do and always have. Maybe it's because it's convenient; the idea of bending down sounds like an additional step that my ADHD brain can't take. Perhaps it's a form of exercise that I have to convince myself that I am doing; I mean, there's got to be some caloric burn happening here, right? Like I said, I don't know why I do it, but I do. Once my son could balance well enough, he also picked items off the floor with his feet, and that's when it hit me. I was doing this because I saw someone do it, and it occurred so early in my development that I can't pinpoint to whom; but with my son, I knew exactly where he got this idea. Fast forward a few years, and he is still picking up items with his toes, just like I still do.

I have attempted to help him not do that. I honestly don't even know why I tried it at first, but I still would correct him and say, "Pick that up with your hands." However, the hypocrisy of this is I was still engaging in a behavior that I did not want him to do. There was no way I could truly eliminate behavior that I was reinforcing and engaging with daily. You see, children love to model parents; we are their first teachers, and it's us who tell them how to do things. They are always picking up mannerisms and behaviors because they are watching us every day, and our relationship and behavior with technology are not any different. For your child to have a positive and healthy relationship with tech, you must ask yourself, do you?

The PEACEFUL Method

I love an acronym; I learned a long time ago that in order for my brain to keep certain pieces of information, I just needed to create an acronym out of them (see UNIQUE parenting too!). I discovered that my kids also learn and retain information far more easily if it's in an acronym. The PEACEFUL method was created from those perspectives. It is a way to remember how we can best engage with technology.

Electronic Guidelines Using Bea's PEACEFUL Method

- Present and enjoying the moment with family members

- Engaged with family members in conversation or activity

- Available if asked to do something

- Collaborative with the family as a whole

- Enjoyable temperament and demeanor when not on an electronic device

- Friendly manners when using technology

- Understanding that plans can change, and flexible thinking skills

- Laid-back attitude

Setting the Tone for Tech Usage

The PEACEFUL method is designed for use in all circumstances, but it came about from our first big family trip to Park City, Utah, a couple of years ago. This trip was the first time I was going to take two neurodivergent children on an airplane and through airport security. I experienced a great deal of anxiety about all the different possibilities for the things that could go wrong. I wasn't sure how my kids would react, so I wanted to be as prepared as possible. (Do you guys see a theme here? Anytime I feel anxious, I need to prepare; this gives me a sense of control. Whenever I feel out of control, it makes me anxious, and I can't function. This served me well as a child and made me an overachiever; as an adult, it's exhausting. The need to be overly prepared is a direct link to my ADHD brain and how I manage my anxiety, but it is also exacerbated by the fact that I have two neurodivergent children, and I never know what to prepare for, so I prepare for all the things.)

In the past, when we went on vacation, we were in a car with easy access to and control of the environment. This is my happy place, a controlled enjoyment where I can predict all the possible outcomes and have an immediate solution to what problems may arise. Having devices in the car was super easy for us because we could park at a rest stop and go for a walk to break up the drive. However, in the air is an entirely different story, and this was an environment my children had not experienced before. Worse, this situation presented possibilities that I had yet to deal with and had not troubleshooted. I thought about all the different possibilities; the first and most pressing, what if I am separated from the children? What if a home-alone situation somehow happens? My son at the time was limited verbally, my daughter was a preschooler; and that, my friend, is how you insert panic. Fear number two: what if there's a behavioral issue and they can't be soothed? I would be in the air for close to six hours with children that can't be soothed because of their neurodiverse brains, and facing the judgment of everyone else, who would not understand that these kids are not having a tantrum but a neurodiverse meltdown: how could I explain this?

After lots of conversations with my husband and several sessions with my therapist, my fears were alleviated and became more manageable; they did not go away, but at least now I could manage them better. I calmed down and decided that using tech for this trip was going to be the best decision. I also feared the dreaded getting-off tech monster I had witnessed, not with my children but others, which is why I had to think of a way to make sure that we had guidelines and knew how to implement them. This trip inspired the PEACEFUL guidelines.

I have shared this story with many people willing to listen. I like sharing this story because it showcased a marriage, a blend of interacting as a family and using tech, and how tech can be an engaging and fulfilling experience for everyone.

Prior to our departure, and I mean months of preparation and communication, my husband and I had a conversation about our expectations of the children regarding tech. I wanted it to be PEACEFUL; I wanted to make sure we created positive and beautiful memories of us being together and having downtime for our individual leisure breaks. Creating rules for children under five years old is different from that for children that are 6 through 12 and, of course, from the teens at 13 and up. I wanted these rules to have a lasting effect: concepts that can be introduced early but not necessarily followed. And since repetition is the key to learning once the concept is introduced, the probability of success increases with each interaction. While my children were young, I knew that traveling as a family was important to me, and the sooner I implemented travel procedures for tech, the easier it would be.

Neurodivergent breaks are crucial to maintaining peace. Neurodivergent breaks are needed when one or all of us feel overwhelmed with the current environment. We all have different sensory needs, and due to that fact, we do not get overwhelmed by the same thing. I love being outdoors, and I like loud sounds; I can spend hours outside and lose total track of time. The seeker in me loves nature, and I am always at peace outside. However, if I am indoors, I require silence; I get easily distracted by what is happening around me and can't relax. If I sit, I usually see something that needs to be fixed, rearranged, or changed, and I don't feel settled. I feel settled outside and anxious inside. Here's another sensory twist: if I am outside in a city, I am overwhelmed; the sounds, people, and tall buildings make me anxious. I can function in this environment with ease, but not joy. When I am outside in nature, there's both. That's an example of having different experiences in what could be a similar environment; outside is outside, but nature outside and the city outside are two completely different experiences for me.

My whole family has different sensory needs: my daughter is sensory avoidant; she enjoys being outside but prefers to be inside; my son is also a seeker and loves both nature and the city environment. My husband is okay with nature but prefers the city. Sensory twist number two: we also have different nature needs. Mountains are my happy places, forests are my daughter's happy place, waterfalls are my son's, and the ocean is my husband's happy place. Depending on where we are visiting, one family member may not get their sensory needs met, and because of this, we need time away from each other to rejuvenate.

We have been traveling with tech for years now, and my children are in the tween and teen phases. While this age is typically more complex and can present problems, my kids have a good and healthy relationship with traveling with tech. My daughter takes pictures to recreate at home with her art, while my son records videos of water streams or ocean waves to play back when he gets back home. We take our neurodivergent breaks by being in the same space with all our tech, but with noise-canceling headsets that give the illusion of solitude. My children naturally take a break from tech and do something else with ease. As parents, we do the same; we have to train ourselves not to become hypocrites and to model proper behavior. The biggest challenge for us has been my husband, and I. We were not modeling appropriate behavior at times because it is not innate to us. Checking an email on a hike seems like a good idea, but the problem it would create is not.

When you implement changes for your children, the key component is ensuring you implement the same rules for yourself and have an accountability partner. Kids love to patrol adult behaviors; they make the best accountability people.

Inclusion vs Exclusion with Tech

The current culture likes to present tech in a way that is not accurate. Tech is depicted as something that takes children's attention away, stops adults from being present, and ruins moments. While these things can be true, are they accurate? What I mean by that is that correlation doesn't equal causation, and when it comes to tech it's the behavior we have become accustomed to that causes the issue.

Humans are advanced, but less advanced than technology because we need to learn how to manage it. We unquestioningly allow others to dictate how we should manage tech in our homes rather than figuring it out alone. We would all like to believe that a particular method suits everybody in every household, but that isn't the case. The truth lies between what we can do and what we have been told to do; a middle ground exists. Technology doesn't take us away from the moment, our behavior does, and that is what we need to gain understanding of to change anything.

Everyone enjoys family traditions, but family movie time is especially loved around the holidays. Rotating through each of our movie choices and picking the movie for the evening is something we all look forward to doing. I must admit that now that my children have become older, and their movie choices have resembled my own choices, this activity has become the most enjoyable for me. Family movie night is an example of inclusion with tech. Inclusion is not just doing something with another person—that is just an invite. Inviting your children to watch a movie with you can mask itself as an inclusive act. An invite is great: ultimately, people like to be invited, and it makes them feel welcome. Inclusion, however, also factors their opinions into the activity, and in this example gives them the ability to pick what movies they want to watch. The family movie is an inclusive way to embrace technology with your family. Movies are easy; they are something that most of us grew up watching; they're not a foreign concept, and the experience is familiar. Watching movies at home with my family is my serotonin heaven; this experience always puts me in a good mood, and it does the same for my kids. I have no doubt when they have their own families they will like to do the same because it is a positive experience, and this is the case for most people.

What happens when children are older and no longer require your participation to engage with tech? When they can navigate it with little or no parental or adult involvement, and become less available to you as the parent? How do you handle that challenge? Exclusion can be a big issue with two technological outlets: video games and phones. Depending on your household, you may have a problem with just one, or both. Let's tackle video games first.

Video games are not necessarily exclusive. Most of the time, they connect you to someone in another city, state, or even globally. So how can this possibly be exclusion? The child doesn't feel like they are excluding themselves from the world because the gaming world IS their world. They have an active presence in that world. They have an avatar that they have designed, and, of course, there is a community of gamers that they have access to through chats and other outlets. It is not easy convincing a person that they are excluding themselves from people when the world they are engaging with is inclusive of who they are, and they have a deep sense of belonging there. Neurodivergent people struggle with belonging; the 3D world often feels uncomfortable, sometimes strange, and the rules don't make sense. Feelings of rejection by the masses and others' disappointment in them can create a compelling reason to believe that excluding oneself is the best solution—and why not?

Exclusion may not be viewed the same way from everyone's perspective. Playing video games alone in a room might feel like solitude. To tackle this issue, as a parent, accusing and attacking is not the way to go. Pointing out unwanted behavior is not productive with young people. It can feel like they are being picked on for their choices, which creates more division and makes exclusion more appealing. However, joining in with them is different, and not in a weird, creepy way. Yep, as a parent, anything you do with teenagers is going to be weird and creepy. What I mean is to join in with them by asking them about the game and the levels and also asking them about the game when they are not playing it. Your primary focus can't just be school and grades. Children do not share because, most of the time, we do not ask. And when we are engaging in their world it is typically because something is wrong or we believe something is wrong. Joining them also gives you an opportunity to talk about digital safety and teach them about online safety and what to look for. There are so many games available, but not all of them are appropriate for all age ranges. When you join your child in the play, you can help them understand why this may not be a good fit for their brain type or their developmental stage. When I played video games with my children, I was able to learn how they interact and learn the language of the gaming world in which I wasn't an active participant. Gaming is highly addictive, and children are not equipped to navigate around that by themselves. Something as simple as solitaire can become addictive, and I am speaking from experience. Modern games are designed to be addictive, and your child is not capable of working around that; you, as the parent, need to set the guidelines and give them the tools to utilize.

Neurodivergent people tend to have special interests. A special interest can become a hyperfixation, something that you become overly consumed with, and it takes over your life. When kids are young, special interests are cute and encouraged and celebrated. How many times have you heard an adult say something like the following? "He's so obsessed with dinosaurs. We just took him to a dinosaur theme park, and he loved it, and it was fun." What else happens? That child receives more dinosaurs for celebrations and holidays? Well, guess what? Teenagers and young adults also have special interests, but they are not regarded in the same way. At this point, it becomes something that is now a concern. Now it's "They are only into watching this online game, that is not healthy." The only change factor in this scenario is the age. When you shut down a person's special interest, they will shut you down and exclude themselves from you so they can be included elsewhere.

The phone is another way young people find solitude and connection, but it removes them from the moment. When my husband and I decided that we would allow our daughter to have a phone, I knew this was going to be a trial-and-error situation, and I set my expectations appropriately. She was only able to use the phone at home so that I could monitor her behavioral interactions with this phone; it became an extension of her. She could not put it down, and the dings from her group chat notification drove me insane. It made a child with an already heightened nervous system become yet more hypervigilant, which increased her anxiety. Watching her relationship with her phone made me see how it removed her from the present and excluded her from the family dynamic. Even though she was around, her main focus was on what was happening in the chat. The constant presence of the phone made it seem more problematic than gaming on a separate device.

As a true behaviorist, I said, "You are not ready for this interaction with tech," and she was more than okay with that; she was relieved. But what happens when your child doesn't respond this way? It's back to that connection again. Children want to figure out best-case scenarios and negative things for themselves, but when they need help, they need to know they can come to you without fear of judgment. That judgment is going to keep them from coming to you as their parents, and ultimately, they are going to try and solve a problem that they are not equipped to solve, and that usually means seeking the guidance of friends or an app on their phone, which creates more exclusion.

With the phone, inclusion is communicating with your child the way they communicate. I am a millennial, and that means when someone calls me, I do not pick up; of course, not all millennials do this, but the majority of us do. My phone is not for talking: it is for texting, podcasting, and scrolling through my special interests. If you want to reach me or communicate something with me, send me a meme or a text. The only person I talk to on the phone and who picks up her calls is my mom; she is NOT a millennial and refuses to send texts, although she loves video messages from my kids. I have nieces and nephews, generation Z, that I send texts to, and they do not respond because they only communicate through apps. What is happening here is that the generations are communicating differently, and if you do not communicate the way the other person communicates, it will become an exclusion. Let's go back to that inclusion definition again, but in this case, it involves actively engaging with your child's current preference for how they communicate. If they want to communicate on an app, that is what you do, and you will find they will also join you with your communication preference; that is how the phone becomes a way to stay connected without becoming something that pulls the child away. My mother adopted video messaging as a way to engage with her grandchildren, and that is how tech closed the communication gap between the generations and created a space for inclusion.

Chapter 5

Screen Free Zones

Meltdowns vs Tantrums, and How to Avoid Them

Before having children, I believed meltdowns and tantrums were the same thing; I had no idea there was a difference. Not having had to parent a single day of my life, they both looked like bad parenting to me. However, once I better understood child development and had my children, I quickly recognized they were not the same and should not be treated the same. By treatment, I mean approach. They need to be approached differently because they come from different sources in the brain and are motivated by different things. Tantrums are designed to drive the brain's reward center, while meltdowns happen as an attempt to calm the nervous system. When you phrase it that way, it makes you think about it in a whole new way.

A meltdown occurs when the neurodivergent brain reaches its maximum capacity and becomes unable to process any more input. It is an overwhelming feeling of both physical and psychological exhaustion. The factors that can cause a meltdown vary from person to person, and there is no universal cause. Personally, I have noticed that too much visual and auditory input with no ability to regulate or adjust can lead to a meltdown. With my children, I have observed that sensory triggers from excessive external stimuli and a lack of internal comfort to balance out the dysregulation are the typical causes.

Understanding the difference between meltdowns and tantrums and knowing how to handle them can be challenging. Through my own observation, I also gained an understanding that while meltdowns and tantrums happen in all children, they are not limited to children; adults have them as well. We don't call them meltdowns and tantrums then though. With an adult, you are likelier to say, "That person is having a bad day." However, children are not allowed bad days but are categorized as having behavior problems.

I have seen adults throw tantrums over simple things and have witnessed them also have meltdowns resulting from a dysregulated nervous system. Granted, they are not aware that they are accessing their sympathetic nervous system, which is the driving force for "fight or flight," and what they are experiencing is an attempt to regulate an internal system that is causing the outside appearance, masked behind a brio that resembles a tantrum.

Children experience the same thing. However, they must gain the language and life skills to convey what they are experiencing to adults. This is where you come in: as a parent, it's imperative that you are not punishing a child for having a dysregulated nervous system. It is not within their control. Therefore, it can't just be stopped. Technology can help you regulate but can also make you dysregulated. Parents tell me that when their child does not have access to tech, they are different and well-behaved, so naturally, the parents see this as a case of causation, as opposed to correlation.

As a parent, you may accidentally reinforce behaviors that you are trying to eliminate, such as tantrums. When you don't give in to a tantrum, you help ensure that you are not encouraging destructive behaviors that both you and your child have developed over time in an effort to maintain peace.

While it may cause short-term discomfort—like your child screaming or crying—resisting the urge to give in can lead to long-term benefits. For instance, it helps your child understand that there are limits and that sometimes they do not get what they want.

Cycle of a Tantrum

The child asks for the item ↦ The parents say NO ↦ Child starts crying ↦ Parent says NO ↦ The child escalates the behavior by throwing items on the floor ↦ Parents say fine, here you go, to stop the behavior ↦ The behavior is now reinforced by the escalation of throwing items

This dysregulation develops gradually over time, with the pattern consistently repeating. This repetition leads to this new behavior becoming established. Parents often assume that the object caused the tantrum, but in reality, it's the reinforcement of the parental habit of avoiding the discomfort of the child crying or screaming that is the root cause, not the removal of the item

A meltdown is something entirely different; when a child experiences a meltdown after using a device, it could be a classic example of sensory overload: too much too often without the opportunity to unwind from it all. A device is fun and engaging, but how would a child tell you they are experiencing visual fatigue from the screen? Chances are they would not; instead, they would start to break down internally and later have a meltdown when they can't handle it anymore.

Cycle of a Meltdown

The child is experiencing internal discomfort overwhelming sensory experiences ↦ External tasks are presented, but the child feels overwhelmed and is unable to complete them ↦ As a result, the child has a sensory breakdown ↦ A reward is offered, but there is no response from the child ↦ A higher-level reward is then presented, yet still, there is no response ↦ The child's behavior simply runs its course without any external items being present ↦ Eventually, the child resets and becomes remorseful over their behavior

Some meltdowns are unavoidable. They need to happen. However, some can be prevented by giving a child proper access to sensory needs and avoiding overwhelming sensory experiences. With guidelines around tech, you can help your child understand when they are experiencing fatigue with technology and to respect the limits you have imposed as a parent.

As an adult, you can use the same advice and think about whether you are experiencing sensory overload, causing you to experience feelings of being overwhelmed and having a meltdown. You might make a survey of your psychological state after specific interactions with screens to determine if they were beneficial or made you feel lousy.

Creating the Environment

This is the part of the book that is dedicated to decorating...but not really. If I hadn't ended up in mental health, I would have curated spaces for both interiors and exteriors as a designer. When my son was younger, I recognized how important the environment was when it came to helping him understand what was needed in that space. When I started to think about it, I realized how we behave is based on what that space is asking us to do. For example, when I walk into the kitchen, I will open the fridge, look into the pantry, and sometimes wipe down the countertops. These behaviors are tied heavily to the kitchen; however, if I walk into my living room, I will tidy the pillows, fix the couch cushion, and watch television for a few minutes before getting up to go into the kitchen or another space. The downstairs space is filled with distractions that often make it hard for me to focus on what I should be doing with my neurodivergent brain; if I am going to be on my phone, this is the space where I am most likely to do that. The point of all this is to say, whether you realize it or not, the space you create, design, and utilize influences your behavior.

We do not understand how heavily our internal home dwelling can influence our relationship with technology, whether that relationship is tremendous or troubling. In our home, we have spaces designed for solitude, something that both my husband and I crave and enjoy. We have a space for creativity and inspiration that is dedicated to my whimsical, artistic daughter Abby, who is filled with lots of creativity within her little brain. And we have another space for movement: my son, Jake, lives for the ability to move as a sensory-craving neurodivergent child; this has always been the case for him. When we are in these dedicated spaces, tech is not allowed, and there's a reason.

Introducing tech into these spaces creates a different environmental trigger within that space, and it discourages the original use of the space. I did not come to this conclusion without trial and error. Initially, I assumed allowing the kids to bring devices into the space was not a big deal, and they would make adjustments as needed. But what ended up happening was the only adjustment that was made was the device becoming the interest of the room, and the space was no longer being utilized for its purpose. Instead, it became another space to sit and do screen time. I had to regroup, and I realized that when given the opportunity to get a quick dopamine release, your brain will always pick the quick-access route and ignore the slow-releasing enjoyment that was previously associated with that space. Something had to be done and quickly; I was concerned that the association that was being established with devices in specific spaces was too strong, and that this would bring out dopamine and disappointment and ultimately lead to a meltdown or brief tantrum, because needs were not going to be met the same way as they were before.

Here is what I discovered in my mini experiment when I had hard rules about "screen free zones": both my kids were fine with it. You see, I was not taking screens away, I was relocating their use to only designated spaces in our home. They were no longer allowed in spaces that were designed for other things.

Previously, my daughter would bring her device into her art room and watch videos about art, scrolling from one thing to the next; rarely did she stop to make something based on what she was viewing. The original thought behind using the device was to be inspired, yet inspiration turned into mindless scrolling. This is a common trap for neurodivergent people, one we often fall into and do not realize how deep we have fallen, with no real tactic for how to get out of it. My daughter's behavior with virtual art was voyeuristic. The original intention was good; however, the execution was not appropriate for her at this particular development stage. Upon implementing this new rule, her behavior became an impetus towards creativity. I immediately noticed that she would watch drawing and art for a short period of time and then go and try to create what she saw from mental recall.

My son had a different dynamic; the tech-free spaces allowed him to move more frequently and decreased previous self-regulating behavior like stimming. I want to be clear: I have never nor will I ever stop my son from stimming. Stimming is his natural way of regulating his internal system; I quickly realized how important it is for the neurodivergent brain to have the ability to have these short movements and sometimes long outbursts of energy. Previously, it was as if the device was suppressing these bursts of energy from being released because he was sedentary. When he was done with screen time, I saw a considerable increase in stimming behavior that would last for hours; at times, it appeared that it was too much for him to han-dle. The decrease in stimming correlated directly with constant moving and releasing energy, so there was no stored-up and backed-up stimming in his system. The release was occurring naturally, just by being in spaces that were not distracting his brain from doing what it was designed to do. His self-regulation when using devices has also changed. I noticed that in the space where tech roams freely, while he is watching a movie or playing a game, he will stop and take a break; the device will be put down, and he will move. His brain understands the value of movement, which he was unaware of when we did not have screen-free spaces.

For the adults, it was more complicated to implement this because, as the saying goes, you can't teach an old dog new tricks. And boy, did we struggle. We can easily justify why we bring our phones into every room. As a true behaviorist, I wanted to observe our behavior with phones in different settings throughout our home. As adults, we don't have anyone to hold us accountable for certain behaviors, and when your spouse or partner points out what you are doing, you are more likely to react negatively by becoming defensive than you are to change that behavior. I observed that our phones were always on our person and would follow us from room to room. There was not a space inside or outside the house that the phone had yet to visit. I wanted this to be different.

In our household, we uphold the principle that electronic devices should not be regarded as extensions of our bodies. Instead, they are utilized in a manner similar to other devices, for specific periods of time, before being returned to their designated storage locations. For instance, when undertaking household vacuuming, the vacuum cleaner is retrieved and subsequently returned to its closet storage upon completion of the task. It is my intention to instill in my children the same disassociation with screens, for which reason we introduced an electronic charging station as a tool to reinforce this habit. The charging station not only functions as a location for device recharging, but also as a designated area where devices are placed during communal activities such as meal times, family gatherings, outdoor pursuits, game nights, movie sessions, and neighborhood walks.

Since we have our designated electronic charging station where all portable devices live, I had to ensure that the adults adhere to the rules as well, at least for specific periods, and think of it as a downtime for electronics. My deeply ADHD brain craves the ability to access random information, and this was a challenge for me, especially during the daytime when my brain finds it most difficult to stay focused and not to become distracted. Something I had to do in order for me to detox myself from constant distractions was to wear clothing with no pockets. I know, I know, what am I talking about? Well, it turns out that in the home I only wore things that had pockets, so I could house my phone in them. I mean, think about it: you are not likely to hold your phone in your hand as you go from room to room, but you will put it in your back pocket. I need hacks in my life to keep me from doing things that are unproductive and time-consuming. This is my neurodivergent hack; as a neurodivergent person, if it's not convenient, you will likely lose interest and move on to something else. I know I did. The other important factor is, as someone who can't ever recall where anything is—hello short-term memory and ADHD—having my phone in the same place every time has freed up so much mental space and eased my cognitive task burden.

ADHD and short-term memory are best friends; I enter a room and have no idea why I am there. But one of the excellent features of having spaces specially designed for specific things is that even if I don't remember why I entered the room, I usually end up doing something creative in that space. Once I recognized that as adults we had to change our behavior and implement things to help fill in those mental blocks we had, it was a game changer. We find that connecting with our kids is more accessible when the space is built for that, and these spaces are also adult-friendly. Okay, here is Bea, the designer, again. I intentionally created the spaces to be inclusive of all our needs. The spaces are designed to help us all walk into them and forthwith feel like we want to be here and not think about devices.

Our favorite spot to connect as a family is the library; this space is designed for:

- drawing
- relaxing
- crafting
- puzzles
- creating
- board games
- thinking

- reading

- listening to music

- doing nothing

- sitting in silence.

A key point to remember is that screen-free is not tech-free. In order for me to fully unwind, I require some auditory stimulation, and it also helps me focus. I have two preferred methods of eliciting concentration, and they are opposites. On one end, I like total silence. Silence is loud to me, and the loudness of silence allows my brain to go into hyperfocus mode, enabling me to be productive. The other way for me to focus is strident music, an unhealthy amount that irritates others, particularly my noise-aversive family members. This helps me execute physical tasks with zero struggles. The screen-free spaces do not have screens, but the AIs and devices in the space allow me to listen to music loudly or quietly without visual distractions.

Our screen-free space is the most requested family time. The close second is movie time. While we love connecting with children, sometimes we require a connection that is easier to do after a long, mentally challenging or exhausting day of adulting; while movies tend to be the second option, I find that having this backup works for our neurodiverse family. Sometimes, I want to be around my children but I do not have the capability to engage in activity, and movies give me that option. However, this screen-free space also allows us to focus more on connecting and doing things collaboratively; whether we are putting a puzzle together or playing a board game, it's a place where parents and children come to connect. The library is the most used space in our home, designed with all of us in mind. It's the one space that all of us enjoy equally. The decor is simultaneously welcoming and calming; there's intentionality throughout the space to elicit feelings of calmness and togetherness. The space is designed to help us disconnect from our devices, reconnect with our other senses, and explore serotonin-releasing activities that will create a sense of happiness and well-being and, additionally, create memories and traditions to last a lifetime.

I did not always have all this space to rearrange and play with; in our previous 1500-square-foot home, I would put a tent in a corner, and that served as the space for disconnect. My son loved that tent; he used it for years. The small and intimate space gave him the ability to have a sensory break from us. So, if you are limited on space, you can still create something that is going to work for you and your family.

Chapter 6

Screen Time Rules

Some neurodivergent children love rules. My kids thrive with them; it gives them a sense of peace. I have noticed that most children love having rules and experience fewer family conflicts when the rules are clear and consistent. Rules represent the familiar something that you have seen over and over again, and that is consistent and predictable. When things are predicted, they can decrease anxiety, therefore decreasing negative behavior. However, when things are unpredictable and chaotic, that can cause internal dysfunction, which is when you notice a child's behavior. As an adult, I frequently gravitate towards environments characterized by consistency, avoiding those that exude chaos and unpredictability. I surveyed other adults, and the results from my mini-survey were conclusive: we all like rules; however, we also like to test them to ensure they are working.

To some, rules represent clear guidelines and expectations of things they can and cannot do. This is not unique to neurodivergent children but to people in general. As a society, we are governed by rules and regulations, some of which have developed out of necessity and safety, while others maintain order and keep chaos low. The typical home environment is not usually

Neurodiversity and Technology

filled with rules, and most of us don't think about them. I have found that most parents believe they do not need rules because children will automatically know what to do and not cross the line. This belief is what will get your child into a situation that may cause both parent and child to feel disappointment and frustration.

Kids are designed to break the rules and test boundaries. That is the only way they learn and adjust for future decisions they will have to make. When you hand a child a device without rules, that act itself will create a foundation for issues when you want to enforce rules. To a pre-teen or teen who never had restrictions with their technology, if all of a sudden, because of an incident, you want to impose boundaries, it is going to feel like a punishment, and when a child feels like they are being punished, they will naturally resist. There will be a ton of battles when it comes to child-rearing, but this does not have to be one of them; if you start early enough, you can set the tone for the type of relationship you want your child to have with electronics. If you unfortunately did not get the opportunity to start young, that is okay. You can always do a detox. A device detox means that you will take a break for a period of time before resuming devices. This will create a form of reset for both your child's brain and your habits, and help them create something new and effective. You can start a detox over the weekend and, after the detox, present the child with a list of rules, or contract, to let them know that there are new expectations. It will be difficult, and you will get pushback, but you will also get the opportunity to change your child's relationship with their devices, and hopefully yours too.

A contract should consistently be implemented before

handing a child a device, and the expectations should be clear, to decrease negative interactions about devices and struggles that you may experience in the future. For the majority of us, at some point in life, we entered a contract and signed and agreed to the terms. We may not have fully understood all the language and what we signed up for, but it was certainly clear that we were in a contract, and that there were consequences for breaking certain rules within that contract.

The neurodivergent brain, at times, requires a clear understanding of expectations, and with the possibility of executive dysfunction issues, having clear guidelines in the form of a contract is important. Some of the key components that I discovered are important for a contract with your child are the following:

- Behavior expectations: Children should understand how their behavior will impact the frequency with which they can use their technology. The loss of tech should not be something done out of frustration and anguish without prior warning. A child should always know under what circumstances they could lose a device.

- Expectations at school: Most parents agree that a child's job is at school. Schoolwork is typically the battleground for tech. Children should have an understanding of what the parent expects from an academic perspective. Communication about grades should be constructive, discussing what the child does well and how they might address their weaker areas, rather than criticizing poor grades.

- Expectations at home for morning routine/afternoon/evening: There need to be conversations about chores for the morning, afternoon, and evening, as well as the weekend. Devices are often used as a way to unwind from the day or from school, and your child may not choose a chore over a device.

- Expectations for electronics: Communication about the length of time and duration as well as how electronics can be utilized.

- Consequences: What happens when a child breaks a rule pertaining to electronics, and what do they need to do to recover their device if it has been removed from them?

- Children's responsibilities: These are the "tax" your children pay for the privilege of having a device. The child will be responsible for the device, and must be able to tackle this level of responsibility.

- Parent's responsibilities: These are the promises that the parent makes and will adhere to, so the child understands they are entering a two-way relationship where both they and their parent(s) have responsibilities.

- An overview of the child's rights and responsibilities.

The sample contract below is based loosely on the one we use in our household—parents should tailor it to suit their own family.

SAMPLE ELECTRONIC CONTRACT

This contract is an agreement that you are entering to obtain the privilege of a device. This agreement is designed to eliminate confusion and frustrations about what is expected when having an electronic device. This contract is designed to streamline communication from parent to child and enhance the child's autonomy when making certain decisions about their future with technology. While the best intentions went into covering the typical situations that may incur with tech usage, it is important to state that not every possible situation could be covered. However, efforts have been made to cover the general rules and values we are all expected to abide by. This contract may need to be reviewed and altered over time. Parents can make changes if they discover the agreed-upon rules are not working for the family, and kids may present opinions in a family meeting to discuss.

Behavior Expectations

Disrespectful language or behavior towards teachers/friends/siblings/parents/adults/etc. results in two warnings. The first warning is intended to draw attention to the disrespectful behavior, to identify it, and hopefully remedy it. At the second warning, the violator will lose a privilege (as defined by an adult) until they can demonstrate appropriate behavior for a period determined by the adult. Continued disrespectful behavior will result in additional loss of privileges until the violator can demonstrate respectful behavior for as long as the parent determines.

Warning Rule

- The first warning is intended to draw attention to the disrespectful behavior.

- The second warning is that the violator will lose a privilege.

- Continued disrespectful behavior will result in additional loss of privileges.

- Possible consequences:

  > Loss of TV time

  > Loss of video games

  > Loss of computer time/internet access

  > Loss of personal media device

  > Going to bed early

  > Doing additional chores

  > Not earning favored activity

  > Loss of free time

  > Ending an activity early

Expectations at School

- Students should try to participate in class constructively.

- Assignments are turned in complete and on time.

- Students respect all classroom policies and behavior expectations for teachers and students.

- If a student struggles with a particular subject or topic, they must reach out to parents and/or teachers for help.

- Parents will be available to help when asked.

- Any violation at school will have a follow-up at home with a consequence.

Expectations for Home

- Electronics are not allowed until 11:30 am, and only if the morning routine is complete.

- Electronics are not allowed until the afternoon routine is complete.

- Electronic use may be resumed once homework for the day is complete and parents allow.

- All family members shall participate in household chores.

- Chores are considered "complete" upon approval by a parent.

- NO ELECTRONICS past 7:00 pm on school nights, 9:00 pm if no school the next day.

Expectations for Electronics

- Having electronics is a privilege.

- If something happens to a child's electronics, that child will be responsible for the replacement costs or repairs, and the child will do additional chores to come up with ways to pay for repairs.

- Parents will always know the password for all devices and any apps.

- Parents will monitor a phone regularly, including text messages, browsing history, videos, and apps.

- Do not give out ANY personal information without permission.

- Do not announce private family information.

- Do not use technology to deceive or lie to others.

- Do not use electronics or social media to be a bully.

- Don't record audio or video of people without their knowledge.

- Keep personal parts of your body out of screens.

- Electronics are used in shared spaces at acceptable times.

- Turn off electronics during meals and at the specified time each night.

Device Consequences

- Not turning off a device when asked the first time means the device is turned over to a parent and removed for 10 minutes, after the second time for 20 minutes, and a third time will result in the loss of the device for 24 hours:

- > First request = 10 mins loss

- > Second request = 20 mins loss

- > Third request = 24 hrs loss

- If caught using electronics after "electronics off" time, there will be one warning. The next time, the device will be removed by a parent until the next day.

- Downloading a game, app, etc. without permission results in a loss of screens for 24 hours.

- Damage to a device due to poor behavior or a poor decision will result in the loss of use of that device until it is repaired at the child's expense.

Child's Responsibilities

- I promise to do my best at school and follow their rules.

- I promise to do my best at home and respect all rules.

- Emotions are part of the human spectrum and will be expressed in a respectful manner.

- It is not my parents' job to keep me entertained.

- I am still growing and learning and will try my best not to make mistakes.

Parents' Responsibilities

- We promise to treat our child with respect and compassion.

- We will not belittle, degrade, or insult our child, regardless of his or her actions.

- We will treat our child the way we would have wanted to be treated when we were their age.

- We will create a space for open communication where all opinions are heard.

- We promise to spend a reasonable amount of quality time with our child each day they are with us and to give them positive attention when appropriate.

- We promise to set a good example by being the best role model that we can be.

- We will practice ways to handle difficult emotions.

- We will teach our child to be caring, patient, reliable, and respectful by acting that way ourselves.

- We will NOT be "giving in" to our child's crying, tantrums, or threats.

  [The desire to compromise for the sake of peace is a bad idea that leads to a more dysregulated individual. Compromising will not help them regulate their emotions to get them back to a place where they feel secure, which is the overall goal; in contrast, it creates the opposite. Maintaining the rules actually helps with dysregulation.]

- We will do our best to instill firm, fair, consistent, and structured discipline.

  [As parents, we can easily get lost in an authoritative mindset and not recognize that children sometimes need gentle and strict discipline to execute even familiar tasks. When the child is mentally wrapped up in technology, the guidelines need to be fair. Giving warnings in a calm and thoughtful way is a great rule to set in place for you as the parent to adhere to.]

- We will encourage our child to practice healthy habits.

- Most of all, we promise to keep our child safe from physical and/or emotional harm that may not always be visible. We will provide an environment for our child that allows them to thrive.

Overview of Your Device Rights

- Having a cell phone and other electronics is a privilege.

- If something happens to your phone, or if you damage other electronics, you will be responsible for the replacement costs or repairs.

- Parents will always know the password for your phone and any app, and may monitor your phone regularly, including text messages, browsing history, videos, and apps.

- Do not give out ANY personal information without permission. Do not announce private family information.

- Do not use technology to deceive or lie to others. Do not use electronics or social media to be a bully.

- Don't record audio or video of people without their knowledge.

- Keep personal parts of your body out of screens.

- Electronics are to be used in public areas at acceptable times:

  > Turn off electronics during meals and at the specified time each night.

  > No electronics in the car (other than to play music with the driver's permission) unless the car ride is longer than 1 hour.

- Electronics are not allowed until 11:30 am, and only if the morning routine is complete.

Signatures:

Signature (Parent) .... Date ....

Signature (Child) .... Date ....

****Parents have the right to amend this contract at any time if they discover the agreed-upon rules are not working for the family****

Screen Time Rules

In our household, screen time starts and ends at the same time every day, including weekends and vacations. Having a routine around the screen helps children understand the expectations that we have, and creates a stress-free transition. If the start time is noon, it will make no difference if you wake up at 7:00 am, and screen time ends at 6:30 pm, so if you get home from swim practice at 7:00 pm, there's no screen. Screen time always ends at least two hours before bedtime to help my kids unwind from screens; this means that connecting with others is the last part of the day before going to bed.

Teaching Digital Safety to the Neurodiverse

The most important thing your child needs to know is how to be safe when using devices. Digital safety looks different at different developmental stages, because each child has limited capacity for conceptualizing based on their stage of development. Some children, both neurotypical and neurodivergent, have the ability to perform beyond their chronological age and can fool you into believing they can handle more mature subject matter. However, I want you to remember that the best thing about getting older is the life experience you gain that helps you navigate the world. No matter how mature a 12-year-old may seem, they do not possess the life experience of a 25-year-old and are still going to be susceptible to certain manipulations and tactics by a deceiving adult or older child who wants to take advantage of them.

Neurodivergent individuals often struggle to understand complex social norms, which can lead to them being manipulated and taken advantage of. This can make them feel misunderstood and vulnerable in both the physical and virtual world. The physical world is filled with complicated rules that govern how people should operate. Some of the most common feedback I receive is how misunderstood the neurodivergent person feels in all aspects of life. While retreating into the virtual world may seem like a safer option, it also comes with its own set of risks. Virtual dangers such as cyberbullying, offensive visuals, and privacy violations are all potential dangers that may be difficult for neurodivergent individuals to recognize or report. A study by Shi *et al.* (2022) showed that intrusive imagery can contribute to the development and maintenance of health anxiety, which can be distressing for individuals.

It is important to have ongoing conversations about online safety with children and adolescents. The goal is not to scare them but to educate and encourage open communication so that they feel comfortable seeking help if necessary. Create an open line of communication with your child so that if something that bothers them happens they feel comfortable coming to you and talking to you about it.

When it comes to safety, it is easy to think about concrete things: tangible dangers that we have decided as a society to protect our population from, from the young preschoolers to our high school-aged children; we create guidelines to keep them safe. Would you allow your two-year-old to handle the stove or even hot food? Would you let your tween watch an R-rated movie? How about your teenager? Would you give them the keys to your car without logging the required hours needed to demonstrate safety and responsible driving techniques? The answer to these questions is probably not; I hope it's NO. The same consideration must be placed on devices. Technological advances have made our lives easier in so many ways. Still, we have not learned how to use technological items such as hand-held devices easily accessible to children as young as 15 months. Are devices as dangerous as fire, inappropriate as R-rated content, or as hazardous as a motor vehicle? They can be, but they don't have to be. The dangers of technology are exacerbated by a lack of knowledge, lack of supervision, and early introduction when a child may have yet to reach the required cognitive maturity to recognize the harmful content of the virtual world.

Parents may fear it might be too late when their child starts to exhibit adverse effects of technology. However, we are an intelligent species, so bright that we created something more innovative than we are. But we are the ones who made it; therefore, we can learn from it. Has technology enhanced our lives in ways that have never happened? YES, so let's learn how to teach technology and how to use tech safely to this next generation and beyond.

To gain the benefits of technology, we have to talk about safety and child development. No child will develop the same; we are all on our own developmental journey. When I was younger, I often felt disconnected from my peers. I was too young for some things, and too old for others. I had extreme maturity in certain aspects of my life; my ADHD ability to learn and research information gave me the nickname "little old woman." However, I was socially underdeveloped compared to my age group. I had interests that would mirror those of someone younger than me. I was, however, diligent regarding safety and things that felt wrong. The perfectionist in me would avoid anything I perceived as inaccurate, and I guess I was lucky. It kept me out of trouble, and my heightened awareness of danger kept me from doing things before researching them. I can look back at my childhood and see how my mind was always on a Rolodex of which neurodivergent traits I would act upon. Neurodivergent people typically juggle one trait versus another. My ADHD comorbidities are learning disability, anxiety, and sensory processing.[1] My anxiety, which presented itself as perfectionism, kept me safe.

Horizontal and Vertical Décalage

Developmental psychologist Jean Piaget coined the terms *horizontal* and *vertical décalage*. When a developing child acquires a new concept, universally applying this understanding to all related problems presents a challenge. Their cognitive processes do not inherently facilitate such broad application. This is called horizontal décalage. When a child utilizes previously acquired knowledge to maneuver within their surroundings, they are engaging in the process of applying stored information to navigate their environment. This is called vertical décalage.

---

1   Comorbidity is when your brain can't decide how to be awesome, so it picks a few different ways. But the technical meaning is the presence of two or more medical conditions in a person at the same time.

Safety is a comforting feeling, and not something we think about unless it's been violated. I can see how people believe they are safe within their homes, and the idea of that not being the case can be unsettling. But let me ask you this: have you ever had your safety violated or your trust broken? If you haven't, then you won't know instinctively how to steer yourself away from danger, and that means you are probably a child, and your innocence is still intact. When you are neurodiverse innocent, a childhood interest and perspective can go beyond the early years of development and well into young adulthood.

A 2011 study by Courchesne, Campbell, and Solso stated:

> The growth curves reveal an early period of brain overgrowth in ASD boys and girls followed by slowed growth during later childhood when the normal brain catches up with that of the autistic brain volumes. After that, brain volumes decrease in size in ASD at a faster rate than usual so that, in ASD males, by later adulthood, the brain is slightly smaller than average.

Slower brain growth means that your brain is still developing; it doesn't mean you are not growing, but you are doing so at a different rate than your neurotypical peers. When this happens, it means that you can be more prone to danger than your peers and do not understand how to navigate away from potentially harmful things. It also means that you lack the executive function skills, a constellation of cognitive abilities that drive goal-oriented behavior and are critical to adapting to an ever-changing world, to help you figure out what to do when it comes to danger.

Safety is the number one reason why parents are scared

away from technology. With good reason—it's completely understandable. Technology takes danger from the outside and implements it inside your home; it's insidious. You have no idea it's there, but it can impact your child's social and emotional growth, and physical health, and you might have no idea.

Some parents' attempt at keeping their child safe is to have a "no technology" rule. I don't blame them; if you don't bring it into your life, it's not a factor. But that does not mean your child won't be exposed to it. You have kept it out of your home but not necessarily out of your child's life. However, I have seen parents on the other end of the spectrum who are less fearful and have fewer reservations. When technology is introduced, it is done with the idea that it's completely safe and requires no safety guards. These are opposite ideologies, and both possess their own unique challenges as well as unrealistic expectations.

It can be challenging for a parent to understand why their child can't do something. In order for you to understand your child's behavior, you have first to understand the reason and logic behind that behavior. The difference with the neurodivergent brain is that some essential components of making decisions are missing, causing the person to make certain judgments with a degree of impairment that varies from person to person. When you have executive dysfunction issues, you are going to have difficulties with some cognitive processes.

The brain plays a crucial role in shaping our ability to learn. For many neurodivergent individuals, certain cognitive processes can present significant challenges, leading to heightened levels of stress and frustration. This is particularly true during early developmental stages when individuals may not fully understand or have appropriate strategies to cope with their unique learning differences, and when there is a lack of support and guidance available to them.

Brain Functions That May Be Impacted in Neurodiverse Children

- **Attentional control:** Imagine your brain as a conductor, orchestrating your focus and attention. This is what we call attentional control, a cognitive function managed by the frontal areas of the brain. It's the capacity to select and concentrate on a specific subject, like a maestro guiding a symphony.

- **Cognitive inhibition** plays a crucial role in our ability to concentrate. It allows us to narrow our attention by filtering out distracting or irrelevant stimuli in our surroundings. This filtering process can operate both consciously, when we deliberately block out distractions, and unconsciously, when our brain automatically suppresses unwanted information.

- **Inhibitory control,** or response inhibition, describes how we override our natural responses to choose behavior that gets us closer to our goals. Think of a cookie on the table—you may want to eat it; however, if the goal is to lose weight, you can exercise inhibitory control to manage that response and enable you to walk away. This process involves recognizing the desire to eat the cookie, evaluating the potential consequences, and making a decision based on our long-term goals.

- **Working memory**, often confused with short-term memory, is a cognitive function that enables the manipulation of stored information. Unlike short-term memory, which is the temporary storage of information, working memory allows us to actively hold and manipulate information in our minds, such as trying to remember a phone number that was just given to us.

- **Cognitive flexibility** is a valuable skill that allows us to switch with relative ease from one task to another without becoming agitated or irritated because we were interrupted. This ability not only enhances our productivity but also reduces stress, making us more adaptable and resilient in our daily lives, for example switching from working on a puzzle to getting ready for dinner.

- **Planning** is thinking about activities we want to do and the steps that are important for success with each activity. It gives you a goal and creates a plan to achieve it. If I want to change the doorknob, I need to work out before starting what tools I will need, so I can do it without making multiple trips back to the garage to grab the missing tools.

- **Forecasting** is a powerful tool that allows us to look into the future and anticipate possible barriers we may encounter when engaging in an activity. By identifying these barriers in advance, we can make adjustments to avoid negative outcomes and unnecessary frustrations, empowering us to take control of our future.

- **Fluid intelligence** is the ability to think your way through a novel issue with ease and see possible solutions.

- **Crystallized intelligence** uses previously learned information and applies it to the current situation to come up with a feasible outcome.

There are things we still need to learn about child development. My experience with child development goes as far back as I can remember, from babysitting to finally having my own children, and the pattern that I have consistently seen is that each child is different and will develop at their own unique pace.

My son with autism taught me that I can't rush his development, and my daughter taught me that development can start in one direction but slowly switch gear into something else. According to Feldman (1980) and Flavell (1982) (cited in Fischer & Bullock, 1984), children do not develop in stages as traditionally defined. That is, their behavior changes gradually, not abruptly. Development occurs at different rates in various areas rather than showing orchestrated changes across all domains. Different children develop in different ways. What does this mean? Well, it takes time to learn and practice a new skill or to understand a new rule. That's why creating guidelines and repeating them is essential to help your child learn—it is important for all children, and especially so for neurodiverse children, who learn in different ways.

However, there are certain general parameters that can at least give us an example to stay within a range of what to be expected. Guidelines are just that, a guide, but they are not law, nor should they be treated as such. Having a reference is intended to help you make informed decisions about which direction to move towards or when to adjust if needed.

I have found that the two biggest reasons why rules or guidelines are not adhered to are a lack of consistency and unrealistic expectations from a developmental perspective. Developmentally speaking, rules should follow guidelines that are appropriate to that age. However, even when you apply particular guidelines to your child's age, they may not align with their development. Chronological age doesn't always match neurodivergent children's maturity or development. This mismatch of abilities often confuses parents and makes creating a routine difficult because they are not sure what will be appropriate; I have also seen that this keeps them from being consistent: they are not sure what exactly will work, so they keep changing it.

When I was younger, I was often told that I was very mature for my age, something I took great pride in. I wanted to be mature. It meant that I was "good." A well-behaved child is a good child. However, there was another aspect of me that was immature. I hid that part from most and only showed it to people I felt I could behave in this manner with without judgment. While a part of my brain could access a 35-year-old woman at the tender age of ten years, another could also access a six-year-old given the right situation.

Neurodivergent people live in this world, showcasing incredible gifts of wisdom and insight one moment and the very next having a complete meltdown because our favorite flavor of ice cream is not available: bizarre, right? I think so, but it's pretty fantastic. Imagine having the whole human development catalog at your disposal. I use the term *disposal* loosely. I can't easily access certain parts of me in extreme situations, but I do have that capability. I have seen a similar reaction with my children. When it comes to interests, they both have a high level of maturity in that area; however, with other things, it's frustrating because it appears that either they don't get it or I don't get it.

It's that simple: whenever I put rules in place that they don't follow, they are not there yet, making parenting more challenging. But this is a self-inflicted challenge, and it doesn't have to be that way. In most cases, I have to change the way I look at the situation, make adjustments from my perspective, and not expect them to change. After all, they are modeling me, not the other way around.

I have worked diligently and passionately in my career to teach others what I have learned. I teach the families that I deal with to do the same. At this point, I am a person who believes in meeting children where they are; I also believe in meeting adults where they are as well. Neurodivergent children turn into neurodivergent adults, who also have needs to be met; however, before that transition into adulthood, there are a few steps along the way that we have to consider.

Breaking the developmental transitions into elementary (ages 5–10), middle (ages 11–13), and high school (ages 14–18) is an easier guide to help you understand specific development goals when it comes to routines and tech. As a reminder, your child can be elementary age yet have the capabilities to follow a high school routine, or your child can be a high-schooler and struggle with goals set for elementary. One is NOT better than the other; it is a matter of where your child is and ensuring we meet them there.

Elementary School

Implementation of rules should start in the elementary years. This is a GREAT place to start; it's the best and most optimal because, at this stage, you can see how your child responds to rules and make adaptations along the way. This is why most professionals push early intervention to introduce therapy or new skills to help a child adapt. Early intervention is not the only way, but it makes the later years easier to handle, which is why we recommend it. I have seen that most parents have decent control over their child's early years. However, I have also seen how lack of restrictions sets the tone for a battle. Here are the guidelines:

1. Communicate your expectations: For example, if you give your child a device while in a store, let your child know that this only for the time that you are in the store. The device should be turned off or handed back to the parent the minute you leave the store. If you do this, this is the rule, and your child will understand. However, it's not a rule if you do it sometimes and not others. It's a

suggestion. Once something becomes a suggestion, it's up to interpretation.

2. Explain the consequences ahead of time for not adhering to the rules: Consequences are not supposed to be punishment. Consequences are a direct result of an understood agreement that was broken. A punishment is a consequence for a behavior that a parent responds to out of frustration or anger. For example: The child is at the store with the device, but you didn't communicate the rule to them. You and the child get out of the store, and you ask the child for the device; the child gets upset and exhibits unpleasant behavior, and then you tell the child they have lost the device. The child is confused, and you are disappointed. This negative interaction could have been avoided with communication about what you expect. I have also seen parents not communicate with children who are limited verbally or non-verbal. However, it is still essential to let them know the rule, because being limited verbally or non-verbal is not the same as being non-communicative.

3. Reward with praise and positive affirmation, not additional device time. Avoid doing this: The child turns off the device; wow, you can have ten additional minutes since you turned off your device without a fuss. This may sound like a good idea at the moment, but what happens when you do this frequently enough that it becomes a habit? This is a young child. They follow your lead and will expect this when fully engaged or invested in their

device; this can easily become the expectation, not the exception. Praising children for a job well done goes a long way for positive self-esteem and self-worth. For example, you could say, "Thank you for turning off your device; that was fantastic."

Middle School

Middle schoolers are engaging; they grasp and understand rules and will test some boundaries, but not all of them. In this stage, the goal is to have a Q&A exchange with your child. You would want them to have an understanding but still want to ask permission for things without going rogue. Guidelines in this stage are:

1. Communicate your expectations.

2. Explain the consequences ahead of time.

3. Reward with praise and positive affirmation, not additional device time.

4. Open dialogue about expectations. Since middle schoolers typically have more understanding, they can question why these rules exist. Kids questioning rules is not a sign of difference but a maturing brain. Part of child development is to move past the previous stage. My son, at a young age, was the most agreeable child; everyone would point it out. While some of that was due to temperament, it was also where he was developmentally. When

he started to change, I was taken back. I know, I know, I should have known better and expected it. However, the mom in me forgot that I was a professional. It was strange to see him say no to things that he would have easily agreed to do previously, but it was developmentally appropriate. I had to change my strategy and understand that he required an explanation; even if I felt like it was not necessary, it was needed.

5. Be open to feedback: Feedback from your child is a good thing; it shows that they are comfortable exchanging information with you, and having an understanding that you are seeing their individuality and respecting them as a person who is growing and maturing. The child must understand that their feedback is an opportunity to be heard and understood, but doesn't mean that there will be an immediate change in the rules; it is not an invitation for manipulation. Children need to feel heard, as do adults; however, they also need to understand that things taken into consideration will not necessarily result in changes. Some rules may change, while others stay the same. These guidelines are created for safety; your child may not understand them but will appreciate them later.

6. Integrity conversation: I have seen the wheels fall off repeatedly during the middle school years, with the dreaded "But my friends don't have to do this." Chances are this is true; they may have friends who are not following these rules or any rules, and this makes your job really hard. When my children were younger and were only exposed to our household rules, we had no pushback.

However, as they got older and gained exposure to other households, it became a constant "but this friend's mom is doing it this way," or "that friend's dad is allowing that." Enter the integrity conversation. It is hard to teach children to do the right thing when everyone else is saying it's wrong. However, here is the truth. We are a neurodivergent household, and there are so many things that other people are doing that simply will not work for our dynamic. I have shared that we do not live in the neurodivergent closet; I have been open and honest with my kids about who they are and their brain types, which makes these conversations easier. When children push back, it's typically due to comparison with peers or thinking they can behave like another person; well, they can't. Integrity, in this case, is holding your truth, and this may mean that if you are a highly anxious person and you have a highly anxious child, they may not even be allowed to have a device because neither of your nervous systems are able to handle the stress of it, at least not yet. They need to have stronger foundations and understand the way their brain works. Time is everything with the neurodivergent brain. It may not be ready today, but it will be; it will be!

High School

Communication is the foundation of these principles; parents communicate with kids, and kids feel heard by parents so will communicate back and listen. Teenagers and young adults test boundaries like they are going out of style. If you are struggling with a teenager or young adult still working on the guidelines for middle school, this is more than okay. Age is not an automatic upgrade of expectations. We would all love it to be that, and for some it is, but not for all.

1. Communicate your expectations.

2. Explain the consequences ahead of time.

3. Reward with praise and positive affirmation, not additional device time.

4. Open dialogue about expectations.

5. Be open to feedback.

6. Have integrity conversations.

7. Boundaries will be tested HARD. I have seen a pattern of parents wanting to put a strict guideline on teenagers that was not there before or had not been reinforced. This will cause a power struggle, which can be hard on the family structure.

8. Ask the child what it is they still need to know: I think parents look at this stage all wrong. I am often asked by parents when their children are going to "get it" or why they don't "get it." For me, the answer is clear: they haven't learned it yet. Parents look at this stage as an act of rebellion. Parents view it as the child waking up intending to fight about a device. I have discovered that most teenagers want to have device boundaries but struggle

to implement them because they were never taught how. They have been told what they are doing wrong but not what to do that is right. This becomes a situation where well-meaning parents are judging well-meaning children. I want you to look at this stage as "What do you still need to know and how can I help you attain this information?"

9. Help them put it into practice: We all need help, and at this stage, your child may struggle with asking for help. Communication is a struggle for neurodivergent people because of the way we communicate. As an example, I had a hard time showing work as a young child; the answer was in my head, so I would put what was in my head down on paper. However, I needed to show work, and this form of communality made zero sense to me. I figured it out eventually; one thing I never figured out was asking for help. I still struggle with this because I believe I do not need help, or the explanation will be far too draining and require too much mental energy; therefore, I avoid it. Guess what? Your teen may be doing the same thing. However, you still need to help them. Showing them how to put something into practice may not be the immediate ask, but it is the immediate need. As a rule, we all learn differently, and neurodivergent people are not the exception; showing them what they need to know may involve different techniques. Try different learning styles to see what sticks the best. For example, I learn best through auditory and visual input while processing in real-time. You may also learn with auditory and visual input but need to process it later before it clicks. This

shows how processing time can change depending on how information is retained. That's just one example of how a person can learn. If you want to help your child put the advice into practice, it works better if you understand how they learn. This might also be the reason why they are still struggling at this stage; their learning style may not have been taken into consideration.

10. Guidelines are guides, not magical crystal balls into the future, or judgment space for the past. I have seen them used this way over and over, but they are guides: THE END; no two children are the same. Guidelines also work better with consistency and repeated attempts. They are not a one-and-done deal. They must be put in place for a while and revisited to make adjustments to be effective. If you have put in the time and consistency and your child's needs are not being met, then it's best you listen intently to your child and attempt something that will work. Sometimes, the answer is not to speak louder but to listen better.

Hack with Chargers

Something that I learned about my ADHD is that if something involves extra work, I will not do it. This might not be the case for something highly rewarding, but for the most part, my immediate response is "forget it." However, when it comes to charging devices, this rule did not apply, and my kids would leave chargers in places that were not easily accessible and forget where they were. Not to mention the number of chargers we would go through because of damages or getting lost. It was ridiculous. I knew there had to be a better way to handle this, and I wanted to figure it out.

I started to think about what I did as a child, and I could not think of a scenario similar to this one, except for the remote control. Growing up, we had one remote, and if the remote batteries died or needed to be replaced, I would either watch whatever was on or, dare I say, get up to change the channel. And if my brother or sister had the remote before me, I would watch whatever they were watching; as the youngest, this was more often the case. I wanted to see how I could duplicate this but in a millennial version. It hit me; the thing I was trying to limit was excess. We have all become accustomed to excess, and the idea of less seems like some type of punishment. Less has come to be seen as synonymous with restrictive, or bad. However, it's not. Less gives you the ability to work with what you have and build creativity. Less also teaches you to be patient and to be grateful. Technology use in some households is the exact opposite of less and has everything to do with excess.

Did we need six chargers? That was the quantity we had. There are only four of us; why did we have two extras? I like buying things in bulk; that may be the reason. Each device came with its own charger, so I only purchased two additional ones, but why? I did not need them. I am an impulse buyer. Was this one of my impulse purchases? But why would I need six chargers? I could not sell this to myself once I started thinking about it, so I needed to change it. It was hard because I had to convince myself that this would work, and the worst-case scenario did not exist because I still had five extras. I imagined the children ripping the chargers and my house apart, something they have never done, but who knows what could happen? So I reluctantly initiated Operation One Charger. Usually, I am excited to implement something new, but with this one, I saw my hesitation and anxiety come into place. We now have one charger for all our devices; yep, just one.

The main reason behind the charger rule was based on my observation. I saw that the children were using devices until they ran low, then, of course, they would charge them, and sometimes they would charge them as they were using them; that one made me go bonkers. I initiated the one-charger rule because I wanted my kids to monitor their use via battery percentage. They did not pay attention to the length of time they were on a device, but you better believe they paid attention to how much battery life remained.

The rule with the one charger is this: all devices go to the electronic charging station at night. If the device is at its designated home, I will charge it during the day, and they are ready for use after school, work, chores, etc. Then, charging is done for the day and the device is ready again for the afternoon. My daughter is rigid with this rule and always remembers to return her device; however, my son will often forget to bring his device back and leave it somewhere else. As a natural consequence, his device battery will be dead, and he has opted out of screen time that day. I didn't take it away, but he did.

My children struggle with executive function in different areas of life, and this policy has helped them because the desire to have screen time is the most significant incentive and helps them remember other things. Initially, my son struggled with remembering to charge his device and would end up doing something else, which was fine by me; however, with time, he started only to use half of the battery life and save the rest. He created a plan that would work for him, and I was completely fine with it. My goal is to give you access to tools, and you are the one who will determine which ones you will need and how you will use them.

The other benefit of the one charger is that it's always present and in the same place. Looking for things can be exhausting, and having children fight over chargers is something that I have seen. I had families where each family member had their chargers, which makes total sense, but some would still lose chargers, and I could not maintain this way of parenting. For me, this is training and building a relationship with tech; unlimited access to anything has never proven beneficial. I will not treat this any differently.

Back to the one charger, it's also convenient for travel. I also have a mini charging station when we travel, and this is where the charger lives. I am cautious, so I travel with a backup, just in case. My husband and I have our own charger at home, but the kids do not question this because my husband travels for work. They naturally assume it's needed for when he is not home. And I allow them to think this.

The one-charger rule has worked beautifully in my home and other homes brave enough to initiate it. It's been years, and I currently have a tween and a teen; this is their way of living. Families with teenagers have shared with me that it works well but is more effective during travel. The goal is not to eliminate tech but to help their brain assimilate with tech and develop healthy tech behavior that will carry into adulthood.

Chapter 7

How to Transition from Screens, and Navigate Usage at Different Times

How to Transition from Screens

In general, transitioning from one activity to the next is hard for the neurodivergent brain. When I am in the zone and focused on what I am doing, I do not see anything or anyone; I want to complete the task, whether that task is desired or not. Once I get in the zone, I do not want to be interrupted. If or when I am interrupted, it derails my thoughts and my ability, and this makes me incredibly frustrated, and I am irritated with whoever caused me to break out of focus.

As an adult, I can articulate that; granted, not all adults can express this. I have seen adults react the same as a child would in a similar situation because they are not sure why they are irritated at the interruption, but they are. When I work with young adults, especially those in college, they want to know how to be able to hyperfocus on school tasks but also for that to transition into other aspects of their lives, like social gatherings. And when I work with parents of young children, they want to know how I can help their children transition from screens to another task without a meltdown. This points out different developmental ages and yet the same need. Neurodivergent people of all ages tend not to like their desired activities to be interrupted.

Okay, so when you finally get motivated to get into "the zone," it's addictive because you don't know when you will be able to get back into that headspace; finding the motivation to do activities can be challenging for the neurodivergent brain, and you know what else, even if it's something you want to do, the desire may still not be there. You feel paralyzed; there is a term called *ADHD paralysis*, where you basically can't do anything. It looks like laziness, and most people see it as such; however, with the mental stress and fatigue that the person is experiencing, it is the furthest thing from laziness. This happens because executive dysfunction and neurodivergent brains frequently experience this miscommunication. So when we finally can initiate a task and get interrupted, our frustration level is almost unbearable. The ability to communicate in a calm, healthy manner is challenging for young children or adults.

Is interruption the same as transitions? Yep, it is for this conversation. When you interrupt me, it is because you want me to transition into another thing, whether to help you look for something, ask me a question, or remind me to do something. All of those fall under the same category in my brain. Stopping what I am currently doing and transitioning into another thought bubble without enough time to prepare is stressful. And here is the magic word, people: PREPARE. When I am in the zone, the only thing I have prepared for is the current task, and I am not prepared to do anything else.

Let's go back to that hyperfocus mode again. Nothing gets me to hyperfocus more quickly than electronic devices, and it can be a simple thing. Welcome to the ADHD wheel of action...

Let's say I am scrolling, and I see a plant. My brain becomes curious about that plant species, so I look up the species. I wonder where this plant is native, so I look up the origin of that plant, and then my brain tells me to research the culture of the people who live in that area. Through my research, I discover there is a link between those native people and longevity, so then I look at what culture has the longest lifespan, and that turns into what factors lead to longer lifespans. Then my brain thinks, oh wow, there's a correlation between lifespan and eating green leafy vegetables, and before you know it, I've been down a rabbit hole of information that serves no purpose. If you follow that scenario and it makes sense to you, congratulations, you are my people. I just spent hours researching information that serves no purpose and could not transition into something else. However, if someone interrupted that process, it would be just as frustrating as interrupting me for something like writing this book. One is important, and the other is not, but my brain emphasizes both as significant.

When it comes to your child transitioning from screens, you need to understand that things can be miscategorized in the neurodiverse brain, and this means gaming can feel as important as homework even though they are not, and transitioning from screens successfully requires understanding that your child needs something to look forward to in order to go from one activity to the next. For me, both my neurodivergent children and I can transition with ease if there's something enjoyable that we are looking forward to doing.

In my work, when I ask parents how they ask their children to transition, they tell me that they tell them to stop what they are doing and go do something else. Well, what is that something else? The response is that it is something more productive, like going outside. How is going outside more productive? I know what they are thinking: a sunshine and movement break from the screen. Yes, those activities are more beneficial, but they are not more productive. Your child believes what they are doing on the screen is productive; if something else were more productive from their perspective, they would do that. Trying to convince someone that the desired task they have initiated is not productive is pointless. Productivity, in this case, is in the eyes of the beholder, and screen time is more productive than going outside and being bored; therefore, it is productive.

A healthy transition will consist of creating a desired activity after screen time. I call that having a nice pillow of serotonin to fall onto after the dopamine has been ripped from underneath you. The biological function of the neurotransmitter serotonin is complicated. I don't want you to think that it is straightforward, but it has functions tied to mood, reward, and learning, among other things. For the purpose of transitioning from screens, we will focus on those three aspects.

If we can get your child to get into a positive mood when they come off screens, the transition will feel better, but how can we do that when the child is already feeling good? Well, they need to look forward to being in a better mood. That is going to be the reward component. If they know a better mood is coming, they have an incentive to get off screens with a reward of something better than good, which leads to the last point, that of learning. When children learn a routine, they are accessing a part of their brain that gives them the feeling of calmness. A routine helps you transition because it knows what is coming, and your anxiety decreases because if you know what to expect, you are less likely to be anxious about it.

Routine: Mood ↦ Reward ↦ Learning

The routine for getting off-screen in my family is family time. When I say screen time is done, it's followed by a desired activity that is more rewarding than screens, and that activity is, drum roll please, Mom and Dad. Yep, that's right, folks. You are a more desired activity than screens. My kids have screen time daily, but we also have family togetherness daily, and if you give them a choice, they will choose family. You probably have your doubts because my kids are young, and how does this play off with teenagers? I did some research on this with my clients and asked my teens and young adults if they would get off their apps if they knew an enjoyable family activity was coming after it. With no hesitation, 100 percent of them said YES. The caveat was that it couldn't be time to clean or do chores as a family. None of them thought this was a good idea or a reason to get off their screens, but if the family were to play a game, go for a walk, or watch a movie that they all enjoyed, the teens and young adults would be happy to put their device away.

My sample size was small, not enough to say that this is a scientific breakthrough, but other research has pointed to this exact thing (see Li & Guo, 2023).

Positive, healthy family interaction is more desired and

considered better than being on screens. When you want your child to transition from screens with ease, you have to have a better alternative: something that is going to make them want to get off their screens. The earlier you start this routine, the easier it will be later on because now you have built a habit that your child can follow. Our family routine is simple: screen time is followed by family-together time. While my kids are on screen, I can get other things done and prepare for the evening. Their devices are on automatic timers, and when they shut off, they put them back in the family charging station, which is when we spend time together.

As a parent, your ability to adhere to this routine will determine its level of success; you have to hold yourself accountable for getting your own tasks completed so you can be ready. Time blindness is something that I struggle with as a person with ADHD. Therefore, I can easily say one minute, but it really meant 30 minutes. I have to hold myself accountable for the fact that this is a weakness, and because it's a weakness, I can't rely on managing time successfully. I use visual reminders as well as environment cues to keep myself accountable; when I see my husband walk through the door, I know I have less than ten minutes to wrap up my task. Look to your daily environment and things that happen like clockwork to help you stay on time.

I also look forward to family interaction time, and there's a reward built into the system for my kids and me. My daughter wanted to learn how to play checkers in family time, so I taught her. She then wanted to beat me in checkers. The reward for leaving her screen was beating Mom at checkers; she could not wait to get off her device to see if that day was the day she would beat me. Part of the routine was that while I was putting the finishing touches on the evening, she would set up the board for checkers. My son loves the movement activity that we do; as a highly sensory-seeking child, going for walks is far more rewarding for him because he is getting more needs met from a walk than he would by being on screens.

Sometimes, we break up the family routine, meaning we divide and conquer. I enjoyed playing checkers with my daughter, but sometimes I would rather go for a walk, and sometimes my husband wants to play checkers rather than walking. We played around with it: sometimes we would all go for a walk, or all be inside for a board game; other times, it was one-on-one, mom and kid, dad and kid, and my children would pair off and do an activity with each other. The point is they have something to look forward to doing that is more connective and rewarding than their devices. I am fortunate to have the ability to divide and conquer and I understand that families look different and not everyone will be able to do this. When my husband travels, and I am solo parenting, the dynamic changes a bit; we typically go to our default of going for a walk, rain or shine; this tends to be my go-to. I have found that just getting out of the home environment usually creates a reset most of the time.

The goal is to start with what you can do and build from there. It will not always be successful, but if you are consistent, you will feel movement, and that is a great feeling. Take the wins whenever possible, no matter how small you may believe them to be, because for neurodivergent families, small wins are big accomplishments.

If you create a routine rooted in healthy, positive family interaction, the transition from screens will not be bad. Our routine took time to implement, and it took consistency and lots of trial and error, but it works for us. Your goal is to find something that is going to work for everyone in your family. Take your child's input into consideration. Take a family poll of things everyone would like to do as a family. If you need help coming up with activities, start with ones that have proven effective in the past, then try new ones that no one has done before and see what they think. The point is to try and do things together so they can have that serotonin-induced memory: science can help you get your child off screens with ease.

As an update, my daughter was able to beat me in checkers, and because of this, she wanted to learn chess; she beat me in that as well at the tender age of nine. It was incredibly rewarding for her when she did beat me, but it was also rewarding for me. She worked hard, and I earned that butt whooping. I did not go easy on her at all, and she bested me! Next is Scrabble.

Tackling Bedtime

The dreaded bedtime conversation. Before you judge your child's habits, have you looked into your own habits or the habits you had as a child? If you are honest, this can give you insight into the pattern that your child is demonstrating. You may not like it, but it can help you understand how to tackle this issue. I have yet to meet another neurodivergent person who does not have some sleep habit that they wish was better or different. Most of them are okay with it, but they have all been interested in understanding how to improve it. I have also dealt with parents, especially parents of teenagers, who wished their children's sleep habits would improve. The struggle in early childhood is different to the teenage years; but while they are different, they are still struggles that parents wish they could get a better handle on and understand how to help them.

Going to bed as a child was not an issue for me because no one told me I had a bedtime. I didn't have a bedtime; as the youngest, I was left to my device, and I decided when to sleep. So, of course, I did have an issue because I was the one who set my bedtime, and boy, was that a problem. But not one I could recognize as such as a young child or even as a teenager. I would go to bed between midnight and 2:00 am. This was my schedule in high school, but even when I was younger, I never slept at a decent time because I could not do that. It was difficult for me to turn my brain off and rest. Before high school, the earliest would probably have been 10:00 pm, but as someone who watched the late-night shows with Jay Leno, David Letterman, and Conan O'Brien obsessively, I doubt it was even before midnight.

Staying up late and watching TV was a problem before we knew it was; I know it was a problem for me. I would stay up so late that I would watch infomercials with dedication; as a child, I thought, man, I need this upside-down umbrella that will not get my floors wet.[1] What was I going to do with an upside-down umbrella? NOTHING, but my dopamine-seeking and highly impulsive brain thought it would be a good idea.

Infomercials were quite addictive for me. I would stay up watching these people try to sell me something I did not need. But it felt like I needed it because the commercials would say

---

1   An infomercial is an advertisement that educates consumers about a particular product, which is lengthy but engaging.

that it was only available for a limited time, and my ADHD and sense of urgency could have been a bad combination. I had no access to money or a credit card, and eventually, the television would turn into a rainbow, and nothing was available to view. I would then fall asleep and do it again within the week. While I could not get my immediate dopamine fix by purchasing the advertised product, this did not stop me from craving the experience, therefore maintaining an unhealthy sleep/wake cycle that I would struggle with for years.

Remember when the channels would stop broadcasting, and you would get that rainbow-color screen, with nothing else available to watch? That was my cue that screen time was done. I don't recall when that stopped; I think once we had cable, the rainbow disappeared, and viewing options opened up. This brings me to my point: when I didn't have options, I went to bed, but when I had options that I found entertaining, I stayed up.

Even today, my relationship with sleep is complicated. I have never been an early bird; I am a night owl. I have learned to navigate this better with age, but growing up, this was challenging. My mind felt clear and crisp at night, and my ability to focus, stay alert, and accomplish tasks worked best between 10:00 pm and 2:00 am. During those hours, I could get anything and everything done, but I didn't always.

Technology and Sleep

Chronotype is a term I wish I had known when I was younger and had trouble sleeping. It refers to the natural tendency of your body to fall asleep at a particular time. As stated earlier, I have never been a morning person; I fit the profile of a night owl. Understanding our natural sleep patterns is key to optimizing our productivity. One way to do this is by identifying our chronotype, a term that refers to our natural sleep/wake cycle. Dr Michael Breus' work on sleep habits is fascinating. I encourage you to take his quiz to identify your own sleep behaviors, as well as those of your child. The quiz can be found via Pacheco and Rehman's (2024) article which explains chronotypes in more detail. According to Dr. Breus, I am a wolf chronotype, which means I'm productive in the late afternoon and settle to sleep best later at night. Knowing this when I was younger would have helped me understand another aspect of my neurodivergent experience. If you or your child are struggling to fall asleep at the same time as most people, it is possible that you are simply following your chronotype.

What happens if you have a neurodivergent brain that likes staying up in this advanced technology age? These screens never have an end time; you can access anything and everything at any given moment from anywhere around the world, all through the tips of your fingers. Infomercials are abundantly offered and shortened to be called ads, and they run 24/7. The average ad is shown every 4–5 minutes per hour of content. For those of you with excellent math skills, you can imagine that that level of temptation might be impossible to resist.

Tackling bedtime is understanding that if other options exist for your child, they are going to choose them even if they don't seem like great options. Young children may not have options for screens or devices, but they can have the alternative, which is a parent entertaining them; this will delay bedtime. Having a bedtime routine will ensure that your child develops a healthy sleep habit that they can follow daily. My son had issues with sleep from the moment he left the hospital; when we brought him home, other seasoned moms told me that he would sleep during the day but be up at night, and that this is normal, but that after a few months, when he could feed more and fill his tummy, he would sleep for longer periods, and it would be a piece of cake from that point on. The pediatrician gave me the same advice, and like the novice mother I was, I believed them.

When we came home from the hospital with our son, he was not just a baby transitioning from the womb to the world; he was our first baby, and as novice parents, we had no idea what we were about to embark on when it came to sleep. I can say that Jake loved consistency from the beginning; he was and has been consistent, though not in the best or most beneficial way, when it came to sleep. From the very beginning, he had some maladaptive form of sleep schedule. But how can a newborn adapt to a maladaptive sleep pattern? Could I have somehow caused him not to sleep? The human body is extraordinary because it all seems to run on different rhythmic cycles. The sleep/wake cycle process is called the *circadian rhythm*, which operates on a 24-hour sleep/wake cycle that is regulated by an internal clock controlled by our brain and can influence your digestion, hormone release, and body temperature. This internal clock isn't established in babies; therefore, they do not have the same ability to regulate their sleep as adults do. Babies, specifically newborns, sleep when they feel like it, meaning when they reach the point of exhaustion or tiredness, they will go to sleep. It is a very short stage in the spectrum of human development but quite challenging to deal with as a new parent.

However, Jake never slowly increased his sleep periods; he

woke consistently every two hours for eight months with no break in between, and when he was ill, he was up every hour, and sometimes never slept at all during the night hours. My story was unique among my friends, who later on turned out to have neurotypical children, but it's not uncommon within the group of other parents I met on their neurodivergent journey with their children. Sleep issues and neurodivergent children seem to be a natural match.

My daughter had a different story. She slept an average of four to six hours from the hospital. My previous experience with Jake had prepared me for a long battle of no sleep, but she was a pleasant surprise, and I was beside myself. How can they be so different? How can their sleeping patterns be polar opposites when they were a genetic match? They were and continue to be different years later. For my son, being on the spectrum explained his sleeping behavior from infancy. Finding information and researching the sleep habits of neurodivergent infants helped me realize that while I had a routine for him, it was greater than that; it was his brain wiring. In order to be successful with sleep habits, I had to be diligent not just with adhering to a bedtime routine but also with making sure I had guidelines for device use that wouldn't impact his sleep. Without these protocols, it was going to be hard to help my neurodivergent child get an adequate amount of sleep. As a side effect, the more he slept, the better I would sleep as well; these protocols were going to be beneficial for both him and me.

When I think about the families that I help, most of the children don't get anything close to the recommended amount of sleep. Maybe it's because the parents are not aware of how essential sleep is and what happens when you go to sleep. People are not aware of the regenerative and restorative parts of sleep. Yes, when you wake up, you feel better, and you understand that going to sleep makes you more capable of handling the day, but what happens when you go to sleep?

Sleep impacts brain function. During sleep, the brain is alert and communicates with other organs. Therefore, a lack of adequate sleep can result in issues from cardiovascular problems to depression. Sleep debt, also known as sleep deficit, is the difference between the amount of sleep someone needs and the amount they actually get. For example, if your body needs eight hours of sleep per night but you only get six, you have accumulated two hours of sleep debt.

As you continue to miss out on sleep, your brain and body will begin to function badly and you will need to decrease this debt. Newsom and Rehman (2024) state that a full recovery from sleep restriction can take a long time. When given a cognitive functioning test, participants displayed worse performance during the ten-day sleep restriction period, then showed a gradual yet incomplete recovery in the final phase of the study, when participants could sleep as much as they liked. The results showed that even a full week of opportunity to recover after the ten-night span of restricted sleep was not enough to restore optimal brain function.

There is a lot of research showing that today's kids are more sleep-deprived than in years past. If you understand the science of sleep, how cortisol, melatonin, and dopamine work, and how to hack them for your kid's benefit, you can start a few new rituals in the nighttime routine to help them get their best sleep. And probably, you too. An evening routine has many benefits to family systems, including helping to maintain hormonal balance. Familiarizing yourself with these hormones and how they impact the circadian rhythms can help with parenting struggles.

Hormones and Sleep

Cortisol

Cortisol is a hormone that is produced in the adrenal glands. Its release follows the circadian rhythm over a 24-hour period. If cortisol is working well, your levels are high in the morning to boost the energy needed to start your day or the dreaded morning routine. It slowly decreases throughout the day so you fall blissfully asleep when your bedtime routine kicks in. If your cortisol levels are too high, it's not just affecting cortisol, but also decreases serotonin, which can lead to a depressed brain. A depressed, stressed brain is not a thriving brain that can take in information easily.

Balancing Cortisol Levels

Daily gentle movements will help you maintain a balance. Stretching or yoga will do the trick. Stretching as a family is an excellent way to end your evening; it incorporates a slow-moving physical activity that helps with bonding as well as balancing cortisol. It is also appropriate for all ages; even teenagers will enjoy this.

Melatonin

Now that you understand how to incorporate cortisol into your bedtime routine, let's talk about melatonin. Melatonin helps your brain to understand that darkness equals time to sleep. When it is time for bed, your body starts to increase its production of melatonin to help you fall asleep, and as the sun or light enters the room, your body starts to make less of it. When your child is on a device, this can interrupt this rhythm and trick their brain into not producing adequate melatonin, causing them to stay up later.

How to Naturally Increase Melatonin at Bedtime

- Get a good dose of morning sunlight to suppress melatonin and kick-start the 24-hour cycle.

- Create a nightly relaxation routine and be consistent with it.

- Black out all the light—use blackout curtains or shades, but get rid of the light. For young children, you may only be able to dim the light. Place the night light as far away from the child's face as possible.

- Relaxation music.

- Sound sleep music.

- Relaxation routine.

Dopamine

Dopamine's main function as a neurotransmitter is to be the brain's reward and pleasure centers. It is released and triggered by activities that evoke enjoyment and is closely linked to sensations of contentment and gratification. Furthermore, dopamine is also involved in learning.

Bedtime with Young Kids

Young children require a consistent approach to sleep to maintain healthy habits. Introducing a device at a young age can compromise the efficacy of a good sleep routine. While the eight months of torture I experienced was a traumatic experience as a new young mom, the consistency I maintained made it more palatable.

Bedtime Routine

Our family bedtime routine starts with turning in all screens to our electronic charging station. This is a dedicated space where all screen devices are placed daily at 6:30 pm. Once screens are turned in, we have dinner as a family, and we always follow "Serotonin after dopamine" (dopamine is the screens, and serotonin is the time we spend together as a family). The neurotransmitter serotonin is produced by the pineal gland to make melatonin, and helps regulate our sleep/wake cycle. If you have bad sleeping habits or your sleep schedule is not consistent, it can disrupt the production of serotonin.

We are fortunate enough to have weekly family dinners together, and we take full advantage of being able to create a positive association by turning off screens. Our children know that when screens are done, family time begins. We will watch a movie together during the weekends, and bedtime is two hours after the movie. It gives us plenty of time to unwind from screens but also not rush the bedtime routine. The last thing we do is read a book and turn on our sound.

Our Evening Routine

- Electronic turn-in

- Family dinner

- Family game time/movie

- Showers/bath

- Book at bedtime or bedtime story

- Non-screen activity such as:

  - Listening to music

  - Recalling the day's events

  - Journaling

  - Drawing

  - Talking

- Listening to music
- Pacing the room (self-regulating behavior)
- Crocheting
- Knitting
- Sound machine

Bedtime with Teenagers

We all know that sleep is essential for human development. We typically keep the focus on young children, and teenagers are neglected; why is that? I would guess it's because the teenager is on the road to becoming an adult, and our assumption as parents is that they do not require the same amount of monitoring that younger children need. I focus on educating parents on what a child's brain is capable of and how to empower you, "the parent," in the best way possible. I want to educate you on the neuroscience of the teenage brain and how to retrain your child's brain for optimal sleep. The adolescent brain continues to mature until the age of 25. Looking at it through that lens, you can see that teenagers require your guidance more than you initially thought.

Hormones and Teenagers

When you think about a teenager, something that immediately comes to mind is hormones. Yes, teenagers are filled with hormones; however, understanding them will help you understand your child. The adolescent brain produces growth hormones, stress hormones, and sex hormones. Hormones are messengers. They take the information from the hypothalamus and pass it on to the body to tell it what to do. Your body needs to cool down before you can go to sleep, and the hypothalamus is involved in both body temperature regulation and the process of sleep, having nerve cells that control the centers that impact sleep and wakefulness. Hormones move via the pineal gland, pituitary gland, thyroid gland, adrenal glands, pancreas, ovaries, and testes, which are all transportation routes. The pituitary gland releases hormones for tissue repairs and removal of toxins during sleep, which is optimal for brain function. If this process is interrupted due to screen use, this is when your child will become impacted.

Are the Hormones Out of Whack?

Dysregulated hormones can cause fatigue, anxiety, and depression, to name a few. This negative effect will impact your child's development in all areas of their life. Remember, your teenage child is currently experiencing hormone overload, so their behavior may not be an indication that something is wrong but is typical development behavior which isn't a concern.

What's the Link between Screens and Hormones?

Screens can cause too much serotonin to be released, and too much of a good thing will ultimately make it bad. Serotonin makes us feel good, and when you artificially make your brain feel good by watching too much television, it becomes a problem. For example, if you binge-watch a show and feel good doing it, you are less likely to get up and move or take a physical break. Your brain is content; therefore, your body thinks it is also content with the lack of movement.

You are exposed to blue light when you are in front of a screen. When your brain sees lights, it automatically thinks it's daytime, and blue light impacts the sleep hormone melatonin. So, exposure to blue light will impact your sleep rhythm.

Interactive screen time will release cortisol. So that means late at night, when your child engages in a screen activity, they are releasing cortisol, which plays an important role as a stress hormone and in controlling fats, proteins, metabolism, and carbohydrates. When excessive amounts of cortisol are released, your body increases your level of stress and arousal, making it more challenging to fall asleep within a reasonable timeframe, so this is going to impact your child negatively.

Bedtime Routine for the Teenage Years

- Step 1: Deconditioning

  You may have to reprogram the brain to change your body clock. The brain is a powerful muscle, and it's been conditioned or trained to behave this way. These behaviors can include avoiding sleep, staying up late, and excessive screen time.

- Step 2: Remove temptation

  Teenagers still need to turn in their electronics. Helping your child practice impulse control will only help strengthen their ability to have self-control. Avoid keeping gaming devices and screens in bedrooms. Teenagers do not have enough willpower yet to fight that level of temptation. It is estimated that 89 percent of teens have electronics in their bedrooms.

- Step 3: Connect to disconnect

  Create a consistent bedtime schedule and routine. Teenagers are still kids; they want to tell you about their day and connect with you. When your child has something to look forward to after screens, they will always get off the screen when it is time to do so.

- Step 4: Relax

  There are several non-screen options to relax prior to bedtime. I would encourage you to do this together as a family and make it a ritual, giving a natural serotonin boost.

Tackling Schoolwork

The issue of devices and school comes into play around middle school. In elementary school, most kids do not have a dedicated device that they need for schoolwork; for the most part, these kids are mostly using the old-school method of learning, a technology that I guess could be seen as antiquated, and that technology is pencil and paper. I won't cover this stage of education because I have not encountered an issue with elementary-age kids. I'm sure issues exist, but it's not an area in which I have experience or knowledge, so I won't address it: I don't want to tackle this subject with misinformation.

In middle school, kids are getting a high dosage of electronic devices; this is when parents give them phones, and depending on the school, they may also be assigned devices at school and can take them home. When a child receives a device from school, they have to sign a contract, and as a parent, you have to ensure you are adhering to the contractual obligations. Partner up with the school and ask about what kids are allowed to do with these devices and what parental blocks exist to keep your child safe with this particular device. Kids are curious by nature, and they have an exploratory style of learning; when you hand a child a device, they are going to explore it, all of it. This is not going to be limited to the educational aspect; that would be nice, but it is not reality. They have to see what this device can do and what they can get away with. Discussing this ahead of time is essential; it's the same conversation that was outlined in Chapter 6 on screen time rules. The device might be the property of the school, but this is your child, and the rules set at home need to mirror the ones at school; if they don't, you run into the issue of being inconsistent, and that is when you are going to experience bad habit formation.

Middle schoolers are still young enough that they can adopt healthy habits, but they are also old enough to test boundaries. Learn about the devices that your child has access to, even if you didn't purchase them. Keep a communication line open between the school and yourself to understand what exactly needs to be done on the device and what can be completed from a book. When my children entered middle school, they were assigned a device, and the first thing I did was ask the teachers explicit questions about what work was required on the device and what was not. When I started this communication chain between the school and home, it helped me understand when and why they would be on a screen and when they did not need to be. Kids are tech-savvy and can easily navigate most devices; they can surf the web, watch a video, or play a game on any device connected to Wi-Fi, and the temptation to do so might be too great for an underdeveloped brain. The neurodivergent's need for entertainment is something that we know can be a battle. A school-appointed device is not exempt from that.

If your child is struggling with an issue with the device, ask the school if they can have an alternative way to turn in their work. There may be an option you are unaware of that might be a better fit for your family. Anyone can decide for themselves what method is the best, but that doesn't mean it will be the best for your family and your child. Looking into alternative ways to prepare your child will help you handle tech at school.

High schoolers have different tactics and approaches. I have yet to meet a child in high school who did not have a phone. I am sure they exist; I just have not encountered this. In high school, the phone seems to be the biggest battle with tech. Parents complain about their teenagers being on the phone too much or too late at night. The issue with the phone did not start with the phone; it started with a lack of boundaries from the beginning. The relationship your child has with their device is the relationship they have had with technology from whenever it was introduced and the lack of guidelines that were given. The whole objective of this book is to avoid getting to this point of wanting to know what can be done at this stage. The teenage years do not mean it's too late; it just means it will be more difficult to implement things, and the struggle to do so is going to be for both parent and child.

Teenagers are generally social creatures, and the ones that are not social still like to be connected to something or someone. Their devices give them the opportunity to connect with groups and friends in a way that the 3D world may not offer or in a way that causes less anxiety. For a neurodivergent child with social anxiety, a device might be the only way to connect with their world that doesn't feel stressful. They may not recognize that not interacting with the world is causing their social anxiety to increase; they feel like it's helping because they at least get involved, in a way that is comfortable. The brain is designed to maintain safety, and emotional safety is just as important as physical safety. When your child is on their device, they may simply be trying to stay safe in the best way that they can or the way their brain is telling them.

Conversation about devices with teenagers cannot be accusatory. I have noticed that parents tend to go into the conversation with what the child is doing that is wrong but no accountability for how they contributed to the problem.

Teenagers are not adults; they do not have the life experience or the brain development to make them adults. They may resemble an adult based on stature, but they do not. When I speak to parents about this, they are so focused on the age of the child and forget that they are still a child. If you have a child with autism, you already know they are not their chronological age, but when it comes to devices, we want to pretend that that is different, and that they should be able to make better decisions. If you are struggling with your teenagers and their devices, you have probably struggled with another aspect of their development. Maybe they always had a hard time with regulating emotions and telling them to get off their devices caused an outburst. You might think that the outburst was caused by being on the device; however, if you look at past experiences, you might realize that it isn't. It might have been caused by not transitioning appropriately from one activity to the next, which is very different.

When speaking with teenagers, you do get the added bonus of communicating with a more mature brain, but you also need to understand that this is not a fully mature brain. Teenagers can fool you into believing they have more awareness and understanding because their communication skill is superior to a child's; their verbal skill may also be superior to some adults, but their life experience is not, and that needs to be a factor when you are communicating expectations to teenagers. My children are not high schoolers. My personal relationship with teenagers is limited to my clients, and what I have seen over and over again is basically the same interaction. Parents do not go into this with much understanding and somehow expect the child to behave in a mature way. The common mistake that is often made is when a parent says to a child, "I would have never done this," or "I did not do this." This is not a fair statement. As a parent, you did not have the opportunity to do this. Not having the opportunity isn't the same as not doing it; you can't make such a statement to a child. It's simply not true. And you certainly can't judge their teenage capabilities from the lens of your adult capabilities.

Adults struggle with devices; they often have to be reminded to be present or turn off their devices. As an adult, you may not have a meltdown, but that is a part of a mature brain and understanding consequences. A child will not have that same level of restraint because they have not developed it yet. As stated before, teenagers are not mini adults, not in experience and certainly not in brain development; they require the same understanding as a younger child but with more autonomy. Autonomy is what the teenager is fighting to achieve. They want to become adults, and they want to know what they are truly capable of doing on their own. The high school years can be treated like the learner permit years. In the US, when a child is ready to drive, they are given a learner permit, which is a beginner driver's license. Prior to obtaining this permit, you have to demonstrate that you can follow and understand the safety rules of traffic. If you have never driven, and it doesn't matter your age, you have to have this permit for 180 days before you are allowed to take the road test to drive. Now, driving is a privilege, but it can also be dangerous. Driving gives you freedom, and it also allows you to connect with people. I see devices in the same way as a driver's license. They both should be treated with the same precautions.

Tackling Traveling

If you have read anything I wrote in the past, then you know about my love affair with traveling. And I mean all forms of it; ultimately, I love vacationing, and specifically, I love vacationing with my family. When I was a child, we would have family gatherings with our extended family. Now, I come from a big family, and my extended family is even bigger, with lots of cousins and too many aunts and uncles to recall. Family gatherings were overwhelming, and I didn't enjoy them as much as I saw my siblings or my cousins do. I could fake the joy of being happy, but in reality, I wanted time away to decompress from it all; with a family as large as mine, that did not happen. What felt like a contradiction to me was that I had no issues with large crowds or huge gatherings. I attended concerts, I was part of the marching band, we would have football games for hundreds of attendees, and I felt fine. Growing up in Orlando, Florida, and being less than 30 minutes away from so many theme parks, I spent most of my childhood attending events and places with massive gatherings. However, family gatherings felt different. I can see now as an adult that the distinct feeling I was experiencing was the fact that there was also a big social component. I felt pressured to engage and interact with most, if not all, people socially at the family event, whereas if I am at a theme park, I can choose who I interact with and who I ignore. I didn't know this as a child, which caused my feelings of confusion to grow. And when I had my own family, I knew that I would focus on time together as a unit rather than extended time with my family of origin.

I share these stories because neurodivergent people tend

to feel alone and misunderstood even in their own homes. Sometimes, they want to communicate needs and wants but feel like they cannot because of fear of judgment and critique about their feelings and thoughts. Neurodivergent people think that they are so different from the majority that they end up not expressing their emotional state or discomfort, causing more internal pain. My mom did a fantastic job of not forcing me to interact. She was understanding in that way, but I did not want to be at these family gatherings at all, and she did; she enjoyed them, but it was not the same feeling for me.

When I had my son, I thought this would change because I wanted him to be around my family, but I quickly learned that how I felt as a child was still the same, not to mention boundaries were not respected. As the youngest, I had never felt that I had boundaries that people would respect, and they didn't, and nothing changed in adulthood. My family still behaved in the same way. I don't often travel to see my family, and visiting family is not my idea of a vacation. I wanted to give my children options that I did not have. I wanted to allow them to be themselves in all environmental settings.

Now that I have got that childhood trauma story out of the way, I can explain how traveling came to be so important for my family. In my first book, *Our Neurodivergent Journey*, I talk about the experience of my son's first birthday party and how it was a total disaster. For me, the importance of traveling is a direct result of my past, and the experience of raising an autistic son and recognizing that the environment can dictate whether an experience is enjoyable or disastrous.

The first birthday that we had for Jacob was an epic failure. It was one of the biggest mistakes that I made on this journey. His first birthday showcased and highlighted everything that could be negatively impacted when you have a child on the spectrum. Jacob is a rainbow baby, a child conceived after a miscarriage. The idea of NOT celebrating his birthday was never a thought. I wanted to commemorate this miracle child that I so badly wanted. As an extrovert, crowds and gatherings are never a big deal; in fact, I hardly notice the difference between being at a theme park, the mall, or a movie theater. The amount of people from one setting to the next does not have any impact on my senses. I planned Jacob's first birthday with that exact mindset and didn't once factor him into it. Jacob's first birthday taught me a lot about who he was, and I began the journey of letting go of my expectations for him. He was so miserable and cried the entire time. He didn't enjoy any part of it until the end of the day. The following year, I had a smaller celebration; while this one went better, it still was not as successful as it could have been. By the time Jacob reached four years old, I had ceased planning all birthday celebrations for him. I still wanted to have parties, but honestly, it was not who he was. We started a new tradition: instead of parties, we took a family trip. (Moise, 2022)

The decision to make trips came out of necessity for my son and to not revisit past negative experiences that served no purpose. Traveling as a family is our thing. In the midst of all of this, I have to factor in how to travel with tech. When my children were smaller, tech was letting them watch a movie or one of those baby educational series for long car rides. They did pretty well with those, but as they got older, their needs were different, and I needed to meet their needs as well as manage tech while traveling.

Depending on how you are traveling, you can navigate this with relative ease. It's tempting to just put on a movie and stream the trip away. But the key is switching up the tech and taking a few tech breaks along the way. At the beginning of each trip, we review the rules. You guys can see a theme at this point, and that theme is communication followed by expectations. When you communicate with your child, no matter how young they are, you set the tone for their reactions, and you also show them how to interact with people in a meaningful way. I have done this from the very beginning. I was once asked why I talked to my son when he was non-verbal and I wasn't sure whether or not he could understand what I was saying. While that comment was rude and unnecessary, I took it upon myself to see this as an opportunity for education. My response was, well, even if babies do not talk, they do communicate, and parents still talk to them; dogs can't talk, and owners will have full conversations with their pets. My son is neither a baby nor a pet, but he deserves the same respect, and I know he understands. A non-verbal child is not an excuse to not speak to them or communicate your expectations. You would be surprised how much they understand.

From the very beginning, my approach was to communicate what the expectations would be for traveling, regardless of my children's ability to respond. We started this when they were so young that they came to be clear about the rules.

Our Travel Routine

Starting out, my kids choose their screen-time activity. That means watching educational programs or a movie on their tablets or playing a game on their smartphones.

We limit screen time to about an hour to reduce eye strain. Whether in the car or in the air, we take 20-minute breaks with road games, reading, or listening to music. My son prefers to cloud-watch and listen to music. As someone who is terrified of heights, I find the idea of looking outside an airplane to remind me that I am not on the ground is paralyzing; however, my children seem to enjoy this activity, and they get a break. If they are not close to a window in the plane, we have a music break or read a book for 20 minutes. My daughter prefers to read a book and often forgets to get back on the device.

If we are traveling by car, we play road games that encourage the kids to look out the window and off into the distance, inspired by the American Optometric Association (American Optometric Association, n.d.): take 20-second breaks by looking at something 20 feet away every 20 minutes. I do this because I am concerned about digital eye strain and want to ensure I do my best to avoid it.

We are competitive but in a fun and inclusive way. We play games that allow everyone to participate equally. My neurodivergent family members all have different needs, and finding things that are enjoyable for everyone was a challenge, but we figured it out. I recognized this is a reason behind kids being on their devices the whole time; it is something that everyone enjoys, and it's easier, but easier doesn't mean better, and there are opportunities that are missed for family interaction and togetherness.

I came up with this screen-on and screen-off routine to help my children maintain a sense of balance while traveling. When I created this initially, I was the driver and the one making sure they were taking the breaks because they were so young. If you want to start this routine and your children are older, you are going to have to monitor it. Children will not adhere to this willingly because they probably like their current routine, so as a parent, you are going to have to be the enforcer. Initially, the travel with tech routine was created to accommodate a three-hour travel experience via plane or car because that was the extent of our travel. However, as my children have become older and we have ventured off to further places, I simply put the routine on a loop. Therefore, if the trip is longer, they get more device time and more game time, and I am okay with this. We are on vacation, after all.

Travel with Tech Routine

- 60 minutes with screens

- 20 minutes of road games

- 60 minutes listening to music with earphones

- 20 minutes reading books

- Rest stop activity (car)

- Repeat until you arrive at your destination

Epilogue

Technology is ubiquitous, and in our culture, it's in everything. Technology exists in the cars that we drive, the homes that we live in, and the society we interact with. It is in all facets of our existence, so this is not a pro-tech book as much as a pro-information book to make our homes and the quality of experience our children have at home positive. Information on how to integrate our lives with devices is the only way we will give our children some of the benefits we had while working with limited devices and access to screens. In our home, we see how integrating information has benefited our family. My neurodivergent family loves tech, and so do I; the guidelines and information I have discussed in this book have made life more manageable.

How does this story wrap up? What's my relationship with tech after a long journey of over 20 years? I have done some fantastic things in my life and career, and technology has been a constant beacon for me to accomplish great things. Technology has also impacted me beyond my imagination as a mother. I have artificial intelligence (AI) that keeps my life in order with reminders and easy access to information. It keeps an easily distracted ADHDer from forgetting about tasks and helps me manage them. Music access through technology allowed me to write this book; it kept me in hyperfocus mode to start and complete it.

I have also learned the importance of maintaining a balance when unplugging from tech. The only way to access the positives was to gain insight and control over the negatives. So far, tech and I are in a serious, committed relationship in constant therapy to ensure it stays healthy.

I am a dyslexic writer, the author of two books, and contributing author of others. Technology has allowed me to do things my younger self could not have imagined and given me the confidence to pursue opportunities I would not have dreamed of pursuing. I am a mother of a child with communication differences and have seen how technology has given him a voice and given me an insight into his personality. When we started our journey as parents who entertained the idea of tech, it was more for entertainment, but now tech has become an essential communication tool for our son. I have deeply connected relationships and have maintained some of my most profound and meaningful relationships with people who live on the other side of the world.

I am also an educator, and I have spent my entire professional career educating others on anything and everything I have learnt that has indirectly or directly benefited me. I like to learn but have a greater love for educating. The aim of this book is to educate you, and if you apply some of the techniques, it can make your neurodiverse life more manageable and ultimately make my day.

I wrote this book because I want people to have access to information that can ultimately impact their lives more meaningfully. It would appear that each year, as new technological advancement happens, there's this urgency to not fall behind the times by engaging with it or by purchasing the latest and shiny thing; however, there's not the same urgency to educate the general population about how our brain is responding to these changes and how it is affecting our global lives. We must educate ourselves on what we are being introduced to and, most importantly, what we are introducing to our children.

The most significant impact you can have with the habits you create is through understanding the mechanisms and the science behind these habits. It is so easy to think that you have no control over what you are doing, and sometimes you don't; however, understanding what you are doing allows you to reframe your ideas and make meaningful changes that can lead to overall success. You can make essential changes better when you understand what you are doing.

Technology is my friend; it has been so for as long as I can remember. Through technology, I can maintain friendships that are meaningful and impactful with people who are in different time zones, I can connect with others in ways that would have been impossible previously, and I can gain quick access to information that would have taken months to acquire, so yeah, technology is my friend. I also have a great deal of respect for and understand the dangers of too much tech usage and not having limitations on things that could harm my psychological well-being.

The overall goal of this book is to understand the balance of tech and life, navigate this world with awareness, and gain a sense of empowerment. I also hope that you gain some neuroplasticity from reading this book. New information is not always easy to process, and I do not expect you to get a complete comprehension from reading this book one time or in one sitting; this book was written so you can revisit it repeatedly as needed and not as a one-time quick read to fix your relationship with technology.

The information I provide is not meant for you to act on straight away, because that can be difficult. It is designed to show you what you need to know to help with future decisions: to see something that you couldn't see before.

Read this book repeatedly so you can have a continuous conversation with yourself and/or your child about how to implement change and your perception of how the neurodivergent brain processes technology. Let's maintain our neuroplasticity; let's keep learning together.

Glossary

3D world: The three-dimensional world in which we exist and can interact with others.

20-20-20 rule: Every 20 minutes, take a 20-second break to look at something 20 feet away.

accommodations: Changes that help people with disabilities access content and complete tasks, allowing them to participate in regular studies.

agreeableness: Characterized by kind, sympathetic, and cooperative behavior. It's one of the five major dimensions of personality, reflecting individual differences in social harmony.

amygdala: An almond-shaped structure in the brain that helps you process information and regulates emotions such as anxiety and fear.

anxiety: A sense of worry, unease, or agitation, which may relate to a particular situation or be more pervasive.

attention deficit hyperactivity disorder (ADHD): A disorder characterized by difficulties with concentration and focus, impulsivity, hyperactivity, and inattention.

attentional control: The ability to choose what to focus on and direct the attention of one's mind. It involves judging the importance of different options and determining where to direct one's attention.

augmentative and alternative communication (AAC): Methods and tools individuals use to communicate when they have speech or language difficulties.

autism spectrum disorder (ASD): A disorder with various factors that can have an impact on how individuals learn and process information.

behavior expectations: General goals for how we want people to behave in a particular environment.

bipolar disorder: A disorder that includes manic episodes of elevated behavior and depressive episodes of sadness or hopelessness. There are three types of bipolar disorder with different symptoms.

borderline personality disorder: A mental illness that significantly affects a person's ability to regulate their emotions, leading to increased impulsivity and difficulties in managing relationships.

chronological age: The time that has passed from birth to the present; a crucial part of how we see ourselves.

chronotype: Your natural tendency to feel awake or sleepy at certain times of the day and night.

circadian rhythm: Our 24-hour sleep/wake cycles, regulated by the brain's internal clock.

cognitive flexibility: The brain's ability to adjust its activity, switch between tasks, maintain multiple concepts, and shift attention.

cognitive inhibition: Clearing one's mind of distractions or focus on a particular task while doing another.

comorbidities: Two or more diseases or medical conditions that a person experiences simultaneously.

conscientiousness: The personality trait of tending to be careful, diligent, and organized.

cortisol: A hormone that plays a critical role in the body's response to stress.

crystallized intelligence: The ability to use skills and knowledge learnt throughout one's development.

deconditioning: Adapting differently to previous experiences.

depression, or major depressive disorder: A mood disorder that causes severe symptoms affecting emotions, thoughts, and daily activities.

developmental psychologists: Those who study human growth and development across the lifespan, focusing on physical, cognitive, social, intellectual, perceptual, personality, and emotional growth.

digital eye strain: Eye strain caused by excessive use of digital screen devices.

digital safety: Involves protecting your personal data, and avoiding harmful or offensive content online.

digital technology: Electronic devices.

dopamine: A neurotransmitter and hormone produced in the brain. It transmits messages between nerve cells and acts as a neurohormone released by the hypothalamus.

Down syndrome: A disability caused by having an extra full or partial copy of chromosome 21. Each person with Down syndrome is unique.

dyscalculia: A learning disorder that affects a person's ability to understand numbers and math.

dysgraphia: A neurological disorder that causes distorted or incorrect handwriting.

dyslexia: A learning difference or disability characterized by word recognition, spelling, and decoding difficulties.

dyspraxia, or developmental coordination disorder: A neuro-developmental condition that makes it challenging to perform motor skills.

dysregulation, or emotional dysregulation: The inability to control or regulate one's emotional responses. This can cause significant mood swings and changes.

environmental triggers: External triggers that originate from the environment and are perceived through our senses, as contrasted to internal triggers, which stem from our thoughts and feelings.

exclusion: The act or an instance of excluding, such as when a child isn't interacting with their family, but is engrossed in technology in their separate space.

executive dysfunction: The inability to process and organize thoughts, prioritize tasks, manage time, and make decisions.

executive functions: Mental processes that enable an individual to plan, focus attention, remember instructions, and manage tasks, which is not just important but crucial for daily functioning and success.

family of origin: The significant caregivers and siblings a person grows up with, such as their biological or adoptive family.

fluid intelligence: The ability to think your way through a novel issue with ease and see possible solutions.

forecasting: Predicting the future, as opposed to planning, which envisions future possibilities.

heterogeneity: Diversity in content.

horizontal décalage: The inability of a child to immediately apply a newly learned function to different problems.

human development: An ongoing process from infancy to adulthood. Although growth stops after adolescence, each stage presents new challenges and opportunities.

hyperfixation: Becoming completely absorbed in something that interests you, spending more time and energy than intended. If left unchecked, it can disrupt your day-to-day functioning.

hyperfocus: Becoming completely absorbed in a task, ignoring everything else. It usually happens during a particularly fun or exciting activity.

hyperlexia: The ability of a child to learn to read very early; the child often has a strong interest in letters and numbers from infancy.

hypothalamus: A part of the brain that coordinates with the endocrine system by releasing hormones.

inclusion: Embracing diversity and ensuring belonging for all. In the context of this book, it means family members interacting with each other, such as watching a movie together.

infomercial: A television program that serves as an extended advertisement.

Information Age: A period of time that began when information became readily available and widely disseminated, primarily through computer technology.

inhibitory control: Ability to restrain one's impulses and dominant behavioral responses to stimuli and choose more appropriate behaviors.

intellectual disability: Challenges with general mental abilities that require our understanding and support.

learning disabilities: Disorders that affect understanding or utilizing language, doing math, coordinating movements, and directing attention.

masking: Concealing one's natural personality or behavior to conform to social pressures.

Meares–Irlen syndrome: A visual-processing disorder characterized by difficulty with reading.

melatonin: A hormone produced in response to darkness, which regulates sleep and circadian rhythms.

meltdown: An intense response to feeling overwhelmed, resulting in a temporary loss of control over behavior.

mental disorders: Disorders that cause distress and impair a person's ability to function, affecting behavior, thoughts, and emotions.

neurodevelopment: The development of neurological pathways in the brain that affect performance and functioning, such as intellectual functioning, reading ability, social skills, memory, attention, and focus.

neurodivergence: A unique characteristic that defines an individual's atypical traits.

neurotypical: An informal term for individuals whose brain functions are considered typical by society.

obsessive-compulsive disorder (OCD): A condition characterized by uncontrollable recurring thoughts (obsessions) and repetitive behaviors (compulsions).

oxytocin: A remarkable natural hormone crucial in managing vital aspects of the female and male reproductive systems.

pituitary gland: A gland that controls the growth, development, and functioning of other endocrine glands.

planning: Considering the activities needed to accomplish a specific goal based on foresight: the fundamental ability for mental time travel.

Prader–Willi syndrome (PWS): A condition characterized by neonatal hypotonia, poor suck, poor weight gain without nutritional support, developmental delay, and mild cognitive impairment.

procrastination: Postponing tasks that must be completed before a set deadline.

procrastination loop: A tendency to push back the timeframe on a task until the last possible moment and consistently repeat this pattern without the ability to stop or change it.

self-soothing: An individual's actions to manage their emotional state independently.

sensory avoidant: Describes someone who experiences sensory input intensely and avoids it due to feeling overwhelmed.

sensory processing disorder (SPD): A disorder that affects how the brain processes sensory information, such as sight, sound, smell, taste, and touch.

sensory seeker: A person who is under-sensitive to stimuli and seeks more sensory stimulation.

serotonin: A neurotransmitter that affects brain function.

sleep debt, or deficit: Result of insufficient sleep, which affects mood, energy, and cognitive function.

stimming: Repetitive or unusual movements or noises to cope with overwhelming situations.

synesthesia: The blending of the senses, such as tasting colors.

tactile or kinesthetic learning: A style of learning involving manipulating or interacting with the presented information to observe the content. Some individuals learn best with this approach, whereas others have different preferred styles, such as visual learning.

tantrum: An emotional outburst intended to get a desired outcome that's been reinforced in the past by rewarding of this behavior.

technology: The use of scientific information to modify the environment to benefit our lives.

time agnosia, or time blindness: The inability to sense the passage of time and estimate the time needed for tasks.

Tourette syndrome: A neurological condition that causes sudden, repetitive twitches, movements, or vocalizations known as "tics."

vagus nerve: A nerve that controls unconscious functions like breathing and digestion.

vertical décalage: The ability to use the same cognitive function at different stages of development, improving specific functions as they age, such as arranging objects by size.

Williams syndrome (WS): A condition characterized by cardiovascular disease, developmental delay, mild intellectual disability, a specific cognitive profile, unique personality traits, and connective tissue issues.

working memory: A vital cognitive system with a limited capacity to retain crucial information temporarily.

References

American Optometric Association (n.d.). *20/20/20 to Prevent Digital Eye Strain*. www.aoa.org/AOA/Images/Patients/Eye%20Conditions/20-20-20-rule.pdf

Armstrong, T. (2015). The myth of the normal brain: Embracing neurodiversity. *AMA Journal of Ethics, 17*(4), 348–352.

Blum, K., Chen, A. L. C., Braverman, E. R., Comings, D. E., *et al.* (2008). Attention-deficit-hyperactivity disorder and reward deficiency syndrome. *Neuropsychiatric Disease and Treatment, 4*(5), 893–918.

Courchesne, E., Campbell, K., & Solso, S. (2011). Brain growth across the life span in autism: Age-specific changes in anatomical pathology. *Brain Research, 1380,* 138–145.

Fischer, K. W., & Bullock, D. (1984). Cognitive Development in School-Age Children: Conclusions and New Directions. In National Research Council (US) Panel to Review the Status of Basic Research on School-Age Children & Collins, W. A. (eds.) *Development during Middle Childhood: The Years from Six to Twelve.* Washington, DC: National Academies Press.

Johnson, D. L., Wiebe, J. S., Gold, S. M., Andreasen, N. C., *et al.* (1999). Cerebral blood flow and personality: A positron emission tomography study. *American Journal of Psychiatry, 156*(2), 252–257.

Jung, C. G. (1981). *The Archetypes and the Collective Unconscious* (Collected Works of C. G. Jung, Vol. 9, Part 1). Princeton, NJ: Princeton University Press.

Kriete, T., & Noelle, D. C. (2015). Dopamine and the development of executive dysfunction in autism spectrum disorders. *PLoS ONE*, 10(3), e0121605.

Li, D., & Guo, X. (2023). The effect of the time parents spend with children on children's well-being. *Frontiers in Psychology*, 14, 1096128.

Moise, B. (2022). *Our Neurodivergent Journey: A Child Like Mine*. Self-published.

Newsom, R., & Rehman, A. (2024). Sleep debt: The hidden cost of insufficient rest. Sleep Foundation. www.sleepfoundation.org/how-sleep-works/sleep-debt-and-catch-up-sleep

Niermann, H. C., & Scheres, A. (2014). The relation between procrastination and symptoms of attention-deficit hyperactivity disorder (ADHD) in undergraduate students. *International Journal of Methods in Psychiatric Research*, 23(4), 411–421.

Pacheco, D., & Rehman, A. (2024). Chronotypes: Definition, types, & effect on sleep. Sleep Doctor. www.sleepfoundation.org/how-sleep-works/chronotypes

Shi, C., Taylor, S., Witthöft, M., Du, X., *et al.* (2022). Attentional bias toward health-threat in health anxiety: A systematic review and three-level meta-analysis. *Psychological Medicine*, 52(4), 604–613.

Singer, J. (1998). *Odd People In: The Birth of Community Amongst People on the "Autistic Spectrum": A Personal Exploration of a New Social Movement Based on Neurological Diversity*. Thesis presented to the Faculty of Humanities and Social Science, University of Technology, Sydney.

Young, S. N. (2007). How to increase serotonin in the human brain without drugs. *Journal of Psychiatry and Neuroscience*, 32(6), 394–399.

Useful Resources

Ahmed, F., Requena Carrión, J., Bellotti, F., Barresi, G., *et al.* (2023). Applications of serious games as affective disorder therapies in autistic and neurotypical individuals: A literature review. *Applied Sciences*, 13(8), 4706.

Autistic Angels (2020). Autistic Spectrum Disorder. www.theautisticangels.com/autism-spectrum-disorder

Banerjee, E., & Nandagopal, K. (2015). Does serotonin deficit mediate susceptibility to ADHD? *Neurochemistry International*, 82, 52–68.

Bhosrekar, S. G. (2019). *Determinants of Reduction in 30-Day Readmissions among People with a Severe Behavioral Illness: A Case Study* (Dissertation). https://open.bu.edu/bitstream/2144/36039/5/Bhosrekar_bu_0017E_14702.pdf

Boysen, K. (2023). Staying Flexible in Your Thinking to Easily Embrace Change (Podcast). Encouragementology. https://encouragementology.podbean.com/e/staying-flexible-in-your-thinking-to-easily-embrace-change

Choi, M. H., Kim, H. S., & Chung, S. C. (2020). Evaluation of effective connectivity between brain areas activated during simulated driving using dynamic causal modeling. *Frontiers in Behavioral Neuroscience*, 14, 158.

Escalante, D. C. (2024). Psychiatrists and psychologists are most likely to consider socially unusual behavior. London Spring. www.london-spring.org/psychiatrists-and-psychologists-are-most-likely-to-consider-socially-unusual-behavior

Ferreri, L., Mas-Herrero, E., Zatorre, R. J., Ripollés, P., *et al.* (2019). Dopamine modulates the reward experiences elicited by music. *Proceedings of the National Academy of Sciences of the United States of America, 116*(9), 3793–3798.

Ferro, S. (2016). Here's how much kids should sleep. Mental Floss. www.mentalfloss.com/article/81515/heres-how-much-kids-should-sleep-according-new-guidelines

Gernert, C., Falkai, P., & Falter-Wagner, C. (2020). The generalized adaptation account of autism. *Frontiers in Neuroscience, 14,* 534218.

Ghahari, N., Yousefian, F., & Najafi, E. (2023). A family based case control study on perinatal exposure to ambient air pollution and autism. *Novel Research Aspects in Medicine and Medical Science, 8,* 1–19.

Handryastuti, S., & Dharma Asih, N. K. S. (2022). Nutritional opportunity and brain development among fetus and infant. *World Nutrition Journal, 5*(Supplement 2), 15–22.

Jones, K. (2020). Self-soothing in children and adolescents. Is it more than just "a habit" or "unwanted behaviour"? Child Development Clinic. www.childdevelopmentclinic.com.au/self-soothing.html

Luo, Y., Weibman, D., Halperin, J. M., & Li, X. (2019). A review of heterogeneity in attention deficit/hyperactivity disorder (ADHD). *Frontiers in Human Neuroscience, 13,* 42.

Masi, A., DeMayo, M. M., Glozier, N., & Guastella, A. J. (2017). An overview of autism spectrum disorder, heterogeneity and treatment options. *Neuroscience Bulletin, 33*(2), 183–193.

Mazzone, L., Postorino, V., Siracusano, M., Riccioni, A., & Curatolo, P. (2018). The relationship between sleep problems, neurobiological alterations, core symptoms of autism spectrum disorder, and psychiatric comorbidities. *Journal of Clinical Medicine, 7*(5), 102.

Muse, K., McManus, F., Hackmann, A., Williams, M., & Williams, J. M. (2010). Intrusive imagery in severe health anxiety: Prevalence, nature and links with memories and maintenance cycles. *Behaviour Research and Therapy, 48*(8), 792–798.

Tajima-Pozo, K., Yus, M., Ruiz-Manrique, G., Lewczuk, A., Arrazola, J., & Montañes-Rada, F. (2018). Amygdala abnormalities in adults with ADHD. *Journal of Attention Disorders*, 22(7), 671–678.